A MAN
WITHOUT
WORDS

Susan Schaller

With a Foreword by
OLIVER SACKS

SUMMIT BOOKS

*New York   London   Toronto   Sydney
Tokyo   Singapore*

SUMMIT BOOKS
Simon & Schuster Building
Rockefeller Center
1230 Avenue of the Americas
New York, New York 10020

SUMMIT BOOKS and colophon are trademarks
of Simon & Schuster

Designed by Laurie Jewell
Manufactured in the United States of America

1   3   5   7   9   10   8   6   4   2

Library of Congress Cataloging in Publication Data
Schaller, Susan.
A man without words / Susan Schaller.
p.   cm.
Includes index.
1. Ildefonso. 2. Deaf—United States—Biography. 3. Mexicans—
United States—Biography. 4. Deaf—Means of communication.
I. Title.
HV2534.I43S33   1991
362.4'2'092—dc20
[B]
90-46247
CIP

ISBN 0-671-70310-2

Excerpts from "From the Rising of the Sun,": "II.
Diary of a Naturalist," and "III. Lauda," copyright © 1988 Czeslaw
Milosz Royalties, Inc. From The Collected Poems, 1931–1987, first
published by The Ecco Press in 1988. Reprinted by permission.

ACKNOWLEDGMENTS

■ ■ ■

I COULD NOT HAVE WRITTEN THIS STORY without the inspiration and help of Ildefonso himself, and I would not have written it without the insistence and support of Dr. Oliver Sacks. I am also in debt to Robyn Natwick, Jane Curtan, Don Breidenthal, Holly Elliott, Dennis Galvan, and their languageless students. I owe special thanks to André Bohn, Genviève Duss, and Kathryn Johnson for generously providing me with writing retreats, and to my editors, Anne Freedgood and Jim Silberman, for their suggestions, questions, and persistence. I wish to thank Andrea Thach, Greg Castillo, Gregg DeMesa, Carol Harte, Ken, Don, Roger, and friends, Christine Marchant, Tim Baker, Emily Esner, Le Bateau Ivre, La Farine, and the Buttercup Café. And finally, I am indebted to Michael Bloxham for all of his generosity, criticism, and baby-holding.

*To Ildefonso,
who never gave up his search
for meaning and the end
of solitude*

AUTHOR'S NOTE Because the facial expressions, body movements, and use of space—which add sense, depth, and poetry to Sign—cannot be translated, signed expressions translated verbatim often result in awkward or impoverished English. The actual signed expression is much more sophisticated and eloquent than the translation.

In the interest of confidentiality, most of the names in this account have been changed.

FOREWORD

■ ■ ■

Oliver Sacks

ALL OF US, in some sense, take language for granted. Why should we not, since we acquire it as children in early life? We acquire it by speaking, speaking with our parents, without the least difficulty, and without any need for explicit instruction. All human beings acquire language in the same automatic fashion; all of us, that is, except those who are deaf. But for those who are born profoundly deaf, the acquisition of language may be a much more difficult and chancy matter, because they cannot speak with their parents in the usual way: they cannot take in language by ear. They can, of course, take it in, effortlessly, *by eye*—if they have the good fortune to be exposed to a visual language, a sign language, when they need it. But suppose a child is not only deaf but born in a place or a country where education is not mandatory; suppose he never meets another deaf person, is never exposed to proper sign language: what then? He may grow into adolescence, and even to adulthood, *without any language*— a human being, perhaps a gifted one, deprived of what all the rest of us take for granted, deprived of the essentially human birthright of language.

What would life be like for such a languageless man?

What would be the quality of his thoughts and feelings? How much could he comprehend or be a part of human culture and society? Would it be possible for him, as an adult—under ideal conditions—to acquire what he had failed to acquire as a child? These are questions which very few have asked, even the most thoughtful educators and psychologists. And yet they are questions of the most fundamental sort, which could cast a powerful and unexpected light on countless aspects of human nature.

These questions *were* asked, in the eighteenth century, by the French *philosophes*, who were continually exercised by speculations as to how much of human nature was "given" and native, and how much dependent on language and culture. They were fascinated by accounts of human beings who had been, for one reason or another, deprived of a normal bringing-up, deprived of language, and sometimes of human contact as well. One such account was that of Victor, the "wild boy" of Aveyron, who was found, as a twelve-year-old boy, roaming the woods; another was that of Kaspar Hauser, who had been chained in a cellar, without human contact, since the age of three. But these were extreme cases, grossly pathological ones, of human beings deprived of every sort of human contact. Were there human beings who had grown up in normal human environments, but who had been unable to acquire language? A description of one such human being was given in 1798 by the grammarian Sicard, of his meeting a gifted but languageless deaf boy, Massieu, and of the way in which he introduced Massieu to language, and how Massieu, in consequence of this, acquired "a new being."

I had read some of this early literature and been enthralled by it—and then been puzzled to find that it seemed to have no "follow-up": no one, apparently, had explored such matters in nearly two hundred years. Perhaps cases like this had been far commoner in the eighteenth century, when there was no compulsory schooling. It was at this point, in November of 1987, that I received, by coincidence, a letter from Susan Schaller, telling me something of her experiences with a twenty-seven-year-old languageless deaf man from rural Mexico whom she had recently met in California. I was startled as I read her letter, for here, out of the blue, was a successor to the grand eighteenth-century case histories I had been reading and which, I had been lamenting, had no successors. Schaller posed all the old questions, but she posed them in a fresh, and personal, and exciting new way.

A Man Without Words is a beautiful and meticulous study of this languageless man, Ildefonso, and of Schaller's patient, dedicated, and brilliantly conceived efforts to make contact with him and to introduce him to language. The magnitude of this enterprise is hard to grasp—it is, indeed, almost literally beyond imagination; for Ildefonso not only lacked any language but lacked any *idea* of language: he had no conception, at first, of what Susan Schaller was trying to do, or of what other people, so mysteriously, "did," between themselves. He was clearly eager, passionately eager, to make contact, to communicate—but he had no mode of doing so beyond gesture and mime, no concept of the abstract and general powers of language.

Schaller's description of Ildefonso *seeing*, for the first time, what language was—of his grasping, for the first time, the meaning of a sign (and signs *are* abstract, unlike gestures or pantomime)—is extraordinary, and resembles nothing so much as Anne Sullivan's description of how language first revealed itself to the deaf and blind Helen Keller, how *she* came to understand her first word, "water." The first word, the first sign, for Ildefonso ("cat"), was a supreme achievement, a revolution, which transformed his world:

> Suddenly he sat up, straight and rigid, his head back and his chin pointing forward. The whites of his eyes expanded as if in terror.... He broke through. He understood. He had forded the same river Helen Keller did at the water pump when she suddenly connected the water rushing over her hand with the word spelled into it.... He had entered the universe of humanity, discovered the communion of minds. He now knew that he and a cat and the table all had names.... He could see the prison where he had existed alone, shut out of the human race for twenty-seven years.

This first step, this unimaginable step, was the hardest to make; once the idea of language was grasped, its acquisition steadily followed in the intense interaction, the contact, between pupil and teacher. Ildefonso's progress was often maddeningly slow and difficult, and yet it was finally sure and a delight. "His mind was a teacher's paradise," writes Schaller, and one sometimes has the feeling of Ildefonso as a deaf Adam, discovering, through language and his teacher, the whole world anew.

Sicard had compared his young pupil, Massieu, to Adam—an Adam who discovers a new world, attains a new being, through language. Such a comparison is also implicit in *A Man Without Words*, but Ildefonso, though full of gratitude and wonder, is an angry Adam, too, who becomes furious as he realizes what he has lost; that he has, in some sense, been deprived of his own childhood. *A Man Without Words*, unlike the emotionally remote, "philosophic" case histories of the eighteenth century, is full of feeling and passion, and portrays fully the conflicting feelings, the ambivalences, in all their human intensity.

Fascinatingly, Schaller describes how Ildefonso's mental processes, his perspectives, and his very identity are transformed as he acquires language and all it embodies. Schaller has immense respect for her pupil, immense delicacy of feeling; indeed, at times, she is not even sure she is doing the right thing. She wonders whether Ildefonso may not have an innocence of his own, a special pure identity uncorrupted by prejudice or language. And yet she must go on, he must go on; there is no turning back once the learning has started.

Susan Schaller has revived the important tradition of philosophic and linguistic case histories—a tradition that has been all but forgotten and lost, but one which raises many fundamental questions. *A Man Without Words* is a fascinating and important case history; but it is more . . . it is a personal account of an extraordinary meeting, a coming-together of two people on either side of a great divide. It is a story of encounter of a rare and delicate kind; there are aspects of the relation of pupil and teacher, patient and doctor, child and parent, subject and investigator—but it is, finally, different from all these, because the two people, on either side of language, are essentially equal, and what they explore, what they achieve, is a unique relationship, a collaboration between them.

INTRODUCTION

■■■

I ALWAYS TELL PEOPLE that meeting Ildefonso, the hero of this book, was the most exciting event in my life. Until I met him I had never imagined that a person could live without language. But there he was, a man cut off from the rest of us, who didn't even know that such a thing as language existed. He was sitting alone in a corner of the room where I was supposed to be interpreting for deaf students only. A room where I wasn't needed because all of the students were deaf, and everyone could sign. Except those, like Ildefonso, who were born deaf and had never learned a language.

I am neither deaf nor a linguist, but I fell in love with American Sign Language (ASL) and the rich visual world of the deaf when I was seventeen years old. Bored with high school, I visited the drama department of the nearby California State University at Northridge and wandered into a classroom where almost half of the students were signing. The class was called Visual Poetry, a name that immediately appealed to me, and the teacher was Lou Fant, a hearing actor and drama professor who, as the son of deaf parents, was a lifelong signer.

I sat down just as he walked in to begin his first lecture. He signed the lecture while an interpreter became his voice and translated his signs into English. I watched him silently fill the air with pictures and was astounded and delighted by my first encounter with a complete artistic language that used eyes, faces, and bodies in new ways. I didn't decide to learn signed language, any more than I have ever decided to enjoy a poem; it simply held me spellbound.

Fant explained to the drama students that deaf people were way ahead of hearing people when it came to expressing themselves with their faces, hands, and bodies. The course was not to learn sign language but to explore visual communication in order to gain skill in visual expression. His signing mesmerized me. I had never imagined that two hands and a face could be such a stage. As he signed, he looked like a dancer, sculptor, painter, poet, and actor, all in one. I could not take my eyes off him and his three-dimensional art. He was better than anything my high school could offer, so I decided to attend all of his classes. I skipped school every Tuesday and Thursday and walked two miles to the room where I discovered my face and hands and met my first deaf friends. It seemed to me that until then I had never really seen before, or had at best observed the world with only half an eye.

I continued to study with Lou Fant the following year, simply to enjoy this new visual world. I never intended to be an interpreter, but as soon as I became conversationally fluent, I was asked to interpret. I enjoyed being friends with deaf people more than I did interpreting for them, but I loved ASL, and when I married John while we were both in college, interpreting provided a way for me to help support us. Interpreting jobs have also given me some interesting experiences, including scuba-diving lessons, animal-dissection labs, weddings, wild-animal shows, and even working in an operating room, scrubbed and in surgical greens.

In the late 1970s, after John and I had moved constantly for several years to wherever a university for one accompanied employment for the other, we came to Los Angeles where John was starting medical school. I had studied public-health education and worked as a volunteer in mental-health and alcohol abuse programs, but there seemed to be no full-time jobs in the field. In the course of my job hunting, I ran into Cal, a deaf friend and former professor, who urged me to sign up with the local registry of interpreters. At his insistence, I went to the community services and referral program for the deaf where I was interviewed and put on a list for emergency or part-time interpreting. And in this way I came to Ildefonso.

I

■■■

THE MORNING AFTER I HAD SIGNED UP with the local registry of interpreters for the deaf in Los Angeles, they called me with my first assignment. The community college district had requested another interpreter for their newest campus. They did not tell me the name of the class, simply that I was to show up in Room 6, Bungalow D.

I took an early bus so that I could locate the deaf student or students before class began and have a minute to pick up any technical vocabulary I needed if the subject was unfamiliar to me. But before I was through the door of Room 6, I knew that this was not the usual sort of class. Instead of rows of chairs facing a blackboard, there were six-foot-high partitions dividing the room, and everywhere there was confusion. A small group of signers was conversing heatedly in one corner. Beyond them, a larger cluster was doing the same, and across the room was yet another signer. A middle-aged woman at a table was drawing pictures, a younger one was reading a notebook. A man, rocking endlessly in his chair, was staring at the tabletop. I suddenly realized that almost everyone in the room was deaf.

I decided that the desperate-looking woman surrounded by people who were signing continually must be the teacher. Her face was flushed, and she kept turning from one student to another, rotating as she signed. I tried to reach her, but a tall man with an Afro had usurped her attention, slicing the air with his long arms and screaming silently in signs. I thought I might see what I could do to help and sat down across from a middle-aged woman with bright brown eyes. I fingerspelled my name slowly, then signed my namesign (which is a special sign created for each person and does not correspond to the actual name). She watched me attentively, breathed deeply, and nodded. I waited for her to reciprocate. Instead, she made an unintelligible gesture in the air and tilted her face down with the eyebrows raised—a standard facial question mark. She moved her lips as if she were talking but never formed an intelligible shape. "Excuse me?" I signed, and raised one eyebrow to show that I was puzzled. She responded with meaningless gestures, more mouth movements, clicks, and unvoiced sibilants. In one of about every five of her gestures, I recognized a sign. I sat back and watched her mime, gesture, and sign an incoherent story involving sex, blood, and violence. When she showed me an arithmetic notebook and began to write in it, I quietly withdrew.

Then I heard a clear voice and moved toward it. It belonged to a young blond woman in a blue-and-white summer dress and ankle socks. She was talking loudly with exaggerated mouth movements while signing, but her signs contained less than half of what she said. Watching her, I saw that she used no ASL, only English signs and English word order.* She wandered aimlessly, stopping at each desk or intercepting students to give advice and ask what they were doing. "Excuse me," I simultaneously signed and said to get her attention. She couldn't hear me above her uselessly loud voice. Like so many people, she was raising her voice for a deaf audience without thinking. "Excuse me," I repeated, "what class is this?" She signed her answer hurriedly and turned to someone else. This sorry mismatch was named, by the authorities who would never see it, The Reading Skills Class.

Shocked but curious, I turned to help another student. Hesitantly, I approached the rocking man. His shoulders pointed so far forward that his long neck was almost parallel to the table. When I gently touched his shoulder to get his attention, he at once accelerated his rocking. Eye contact was impossible. Feeling helpless and useless, I decided to go home and call the registry. I wondered how long I would have to wait for a bus. Before leaving, I stopped by the door and watched the incredible collection of people. Then I saw him. Suddenly I changed my mind and decided to stay.

He was sitting across the room, alone, and he was

* American Sign Language (ASL) is not related to English, and its sign order does not correspond to English. *I eat bread everyday*, for example, in ASL is: *Everyday Bread Eat I*. Because of the completely different grammars of the two languages, it is impossible to speak English and sign ASL simultaneously except for short memorized phrases or idioms. Signed English is the use of ASL signs in English word order and usually lacks any of the grammatical devices of ASL. Often, signs are invented, usually by hearing persons, to represent a specific English word or grammatical structure (e.g., *-ing*). Fluent signers of ASL may know no English, a little English, or fluent English. A few deaf people and many hearing signers sign only English.

also watching. His back was to the wall, his right shoulder against an orange-carpeted divider. With arms tightly folded into themselves across his chest, he was studying everything and everyone.

His face looked like a painting from a Mexican mural with wild black eyes above high cheekbones and a broad straight nose. There was bewilderment and fear in his look, and something else as well—alertness, intensity, and yearning. His dark eyes, racing back and forth, were not simply scanning the room, they were searching.

The blond aide, frowning, strode over, pushed a workbook in front of him, pointed to a page of pictures and words, and handed him a pencil. It was obvious that he had no idea what she wanted, but he obligingly put the pencil where she pointed on the page. Impatiently, she moved his hand with the pencil across the page, drawing a line from a picture of a cat to the giant letters C-A-T. Then she patted him on the back, looking enormously pleased, bobbed her head vigorously up and down, signed "Yes, yes, right, right," and hurried to another student. He stared at the book for a minute, put down the pencil, and tucked his arms securely back into his armpits, looking more bewildered and less alert.

The teacher called for attention by flogging the air with her arm. A few heads turned to her. "Break," she signed. "Rest, food, cafeteria. Out, all-you, go." Her face was expressionless.

I merged with the traffic and quickened my pace to catch up with the blond assistant. "Excuse me. Hello, I'm Susan," I said and signed simultaneously.

"Hi. I'm LuAnn," she replied without signing.

"How long have you worked here?" Again I both

24

spoke and signed, acutely aware of the deaf crowd around us.

"I just started yesterday. And you? Are you a new aide, too?"

"No," I explained. "I'm an interpreter. I noticed you were working with the Mexican man who sat up against the divider. What's his name?"

"I don't know. I just started yesterday."

"Does he sign?"

She frowned. "I don't know."

"I was just wondering if you had seen him sign anything in American Sign Language or perhaps Mexican Sign Language."

"No. I haven't spent much time with him."

"I saw you were already teaching him some English vocabulary. So he already knows the alphabet. Does he know words?"

"I don't know. Look, I'm not the teacher. Talk to Elena. I'm just helping." LuAnn turned away from me to another hearing woman, talking without signing and thereby excluding the students.

The whole situation was ridiculous. Why had they hired me, a sign-language interpreter, for an all-deaf class with a signing teacher?

I rushed to the main building for a short break. I wanted to hurry back to find the teacher. As I gulped down a cup of coffee, tossed the cup in the trash, and turned to leave, I barely missed hitting one of the deaf students, an impish-looking teenager. He told me that he didn't need school but was curious about this place and decided to check it out. His graceful signs and smiling black face, full of winks, refreshed and cheered me. I answered a teasing question by pretending that I didn't understand sign language. "Lipreading only," I signed. "Happy to-meet-you" and I ran back to the classroom.

I was too late. The teacher was already besieged. The Mexican, who looked Mayan, was still sitting defensively in his corner, his arms locked in self-embrace. His eyes, like a cat's, jumped and followed each movement. I walked over to him.

He tensed as I approached. I greeted him with a gesture and my namesign. He imitated my movements and inaccurately copied my namesign. "Your name?" I signed. Again he copied my movements. His eyes never left mine; his taut arms and face showed his readiness to respond. I sat down opposite him and raised my hands to begin another communication. Immediately he, too, put his hands in the air. I lowered my hands and took a listening position. He lowered his hands and watched me. I began a mime routine that reminded me of "Me Jane, you Tarzan." He repeated each facial expression and movement while his eyes asked for my approval. I held his hands down on the table and repeated my Tarzan routine with one hand. I removed my restraining hand and immediately he continued to imitate my gestures.

I tried once more to explain without language that language existed, to explain without names that everything had a name. I failed, and his face showed that he knew he had let me down. We were only inches apart, but we might as well have been from different planets; it seemed impossible to meet.

I entered my apartment to see empty walls, a clutter of boxes, and no furniture, a reminder that John and I were homeless. Another new city, new apartment, the same old story. The apartment was one long rectangle, dark and small, but it was all we could afford. The same sense of helplessness that overwhelmed me in the Reading Skills Class filled me as I surveyed the mess of boxes. What could I do, and would it do any good? Reluctantly, I unpacked the nearest box, placing a bag of rice on the counter, ten books on the floor, and some mismatched socks in the closet.

As I unpacked, my brain kept churning, thinking about the trapped intelligence in that clearly intelligent, interested man who was so eager to relate. My mind began to race with questions. Who was he? How had he managed all these years? How could anyone understand what language and abstract communication were after decades of silence and meaninglessness? Could he escape his solitary confinement?

John came home, exhausted by his second day of medical school. We were both too tired to be good company, but we exchanged brief accounts of what we had done that day. He couldn't picture a roomful of deaf students or imagine the alienation of life without language. We went to bed early, but I could not sleep. How could I see into that mysterious Mayan mind, I kept asking myself. How did the man think without language? What did he see in all the apparently senseless interactions around him? Could we ever meet?

On the bus the next morning, I tried to formulate teaching strategies. How should I begin? I kept trying to imagine being in a world without language, to conceive what it would be like to have to invent and project meaning onto the world without any information or clues, without any feedback. This man had never received one explanation. Even a year-old baby must have a more cohesive view of the world than he did.

I remembered a dark hallway at Ohlone College in the San Francisco Bay area, where a tall, gaunt man with unruly hair falling over his forehead greeted me with a simple gesture and signed, "My name is B-o-b."

"Good morning," I responded. "My name . . ."

"My name is B-o-b," he interrupted. "My name is B-o-b." He continued repeating this sentence until I walked away. Later, I learned that he had been born deaf, and the only attempt to teach him language had resulted in this meaningless repetition. One of my friends was helping a rehabilitation counselor look for a placement for him, but everyone said there was nothing to be done; he was a hopeless case.

I refused to accept the idea of hopelessness. The Mayan had survived. He must have experienced some form of communication, however primitive. To understand him and to begin to communicate, I must walk outside of language. He acted and interacted with nameless things—shapes, smells, temperature, and textures. To express a need or reaction he must invent a gesture or make a face. I would have to experience with him our immediate, concrete, visible environment. We would have to have something tangible in front of us, outside of us, to talk about. I realized how worthless my first lesson on names had been. He had lived for decades without names, and without having a name he nonetheless had a sense of self. Tarzan didn't need a name in his jungle. My whole approach must be different. When the bus pulled into my stop, I stepped off, ready to discover a link between two alien worlds.

2

CHAPTER

...

I BEGAN TO LOSE CONFIDENCE as soon as I crossed the green lawn skirting the buildings. How wide was the gulf between us? Could we build a bridge? In front of Bungalow D I stopped, looked up to the very blue sky, and drew a deep breath. Inside, the classroom was just beginning to fill up, and the teacher for once was alone.

"Good morning, I'm Susan Schaller."

"Hello, I'm Elena Johnson." Her smile was refreshingly genuine.

"I was hired to be the interpreter for your students, but it doesn't look as if that's what you need. How can I help? Are there lesson plans or assignments I might help you with?"

Elena shrugged her shoulders, smiled, and gestured toward the few scattered workbooks and mimeographed papers. "This is it," she said with an inappropriate giggle. "There are no books, no materials, no curriculum, and no guidelines. I bought or developed these myself. There aren't many good materials for deaf adults learning English, especially on the beginning level. I'm still hunting. In the meantime, I use whatever I can find or think up. I don't know what to tell you. You'll just have to play it

29

by ear until I can test everyone and organize some groups."

"Yesterday I talked, or tried to talk, to the brown-haired woman by the door. Do you know what her background is? Does she know any signs?"

"Oh, Mary Ann? She knows a few signs and is learning fingerspelling; her language level is really low. I think she was raised on a farm and kept at home all her life. She never saw much until someone came by and married her. This is the first time she's ever been in a school."

"And the tall man who sat at the middle table?"

"That's Tom. They found him in an institution for the mentally retarded. He was misdiagnosed as a baby and lived for forty years with mentally retarded people, until someone discovered that he was deaf and had normal intelligence." Elena's voice was without emotion, but she looked down at her desk as she spoke. I couldn't make room for this tragedy in my reflections right then, so I quickly moved on.

"And what about the man over there, sitting next to the partition; do you know anything about him?"

"That's Ildefonso. He's twenty-seven years old and an illegal resident from southern Mexico. I'm helping with some paperwork so he can stay in this country and go to school. He was raised in a rural area and never exposed to education or sign language. He's started learning numbers, but he doesn't understand any signing."

"Since he can't sign, how do you know his name and background?"

"He has an uncle in the area whom I talked to when he registered Ildefonso in this class."

Elena synchronized signs with her voice for the last sentence, because signers began to crowd around us and the office door. The tall man with the Afro elbowed his way in front of me, insisting on Elena's help for a myriad of problems, none of them relating to English, school, or reading skills. As he waved his eviction notice in front of her, demanding an explanation and a solution, I backed out of the cubicle and headed for Ildefonso.

"Oh Susan," Elena shouted after me, "we do need an interpreter in the afternoons on Tuesdays and Thursdays for an Independent Living Skills class."

I nodded and signed "Okay."

"Ildefonso." I was surprised at how much security I derived from knowing his name. My brain, unlike his, found reality more real, more defined, when it was named. I could not imagine a nameless world, empty of all the information given me via a million names and words, and I wished it were possible to peer into his name-free brain.

When I was growing up in Wyoming, I wanted to be an explorer and was afraid that everything would be discovered before I grew up. Now for the first time in my life I could be like my childhood hero, John Muir, at the edge of an unknown world. I would enter and explore the alien mind and life of a wordless man.

When only three chairs separated me from this frontier, a curly-haired, bouncy Mexican woman stepped assertively in front of me, making me hold her open workbook so she could use her two free arms to pop questions at me like a popcorn popper. She was the speediest signer I had ever seen.

"Good morning," I signed with a sleepy face, hoping

to slow her down. I introduced myself and asked her to repeat her questions. Impatiently, she fingerspelled her name and signed a fast "Happy to-meet-you." My eyes could catch only J-u-r-n-?-t-a, but I correctly guessed Juanita. Hurriedly, she repeated her list of questions and complaints about English. This woman's thick red hair matched her flaming presence. She fingerspelled and signed so quickly I was afraid to blink for fear of missing an entire sign or phrase. I hoped I would never have to be her voice in an interpreting situation for I wouldn't be able to talk fast enough. It took twenty minutes to tell her everything she wanted to know about the past tense and more than she ever wanted to know about irregular verbs. Then I scrambled past the three remaining seats and landed in the one opposite Ildefonso, whom I greeted with a smile. He nodded his head a little as his eyes met mine, and unfolded his arms, resting them on the table. Now that I was finally facing his intelligent eyes again, I could not think how to proceed.

He had a workbook in front of him, so I pointed to it and raised my eyebrows in a questioning look. He tensed, copied my raised-eyebrows expression, and lifted a corner of his book. I nodded my head and signed "book." Instead of copying, he opened the book as if I had ordered him to. He didn't see the sign as a symbol but rather as a mime/gesture command, "Open the book." The sign for *book* is one of the few that is a pictograph: two flat hands with palms together spread open from the thumbs while the little fingers stay together. He opened to the picture of the cat and the letters, C-A-T, linked by his penciled line. I remembered Tarzan, closed the book, and motioned for Ildefonso to follow me outside to a world more familiar to him than a classroom with books.

Outside, two sidewalks framed a rectangular lawn with a ten-foot maple tree in the center. I walked up to the tree and patted it with my hand, turned to Ildefonso, and pointed back to the tree. He looked at the tree, then at me, then pointed to the tree. We were equal now. We didn't need symbols. We could simply share the tree in front of us. I tried to think of things one could do with a tree. I patted it again with a very satisfied expression, plucked off a leaf, felt it, smelled it, twirled it, and glanced briefly at Ildefonso. He was studying me, but in a relaxed way. The maple leaf zig-zagged to the ground, and I signed "tree." I exaggerated the sign by moving my fore-arm and extended open hand as high and far from my torso as possible toward the maple. I nodded alternately at the sign and at the tree. I raised my eyebrows at Ildefonso, and he pointed to the tree. I signed "tree" again, and he copied me. He was wearing his Is-this-what-you-want-me-to-do face again.

The lesson ended abruptly as my ears and his eyes were distracted by the noises and movements behind us. Students were squeezing through the door. I mimed eating and drinking to Ildefonso, pointed to the main build-ing on campus, and we joined the flow.

Cup of coffee in hand, I sat on a bright blue chair and enjoyed eight different sign conversations in the lounge. Sign language is wonderful for eavesdropping or, conversely, almost impossible for sharing a secret in a crowd of signers. Once I did see two deaf men build a wall between public eyes and their signs by standing shoulder-to-shoulder, backs to the party, signing and fingerspelling well below their chins. But they were betrayed by the window's reflection. Now the signers in the lounge were uninhibitedly describing their Sunday morning hangovers, family fights, trouble with the law, eviction notices, and failed attempts to find employment. Unable to listen to any more bad news, I turned to my coffee for relief. Looking up, I saw Ildefonso standing rigid against the far wall, looking like a bronze Mayan prince held captive by straitjacket arms. Only his obsidian black eyes moved—a constant vibrato of bewilderment.

How, I asked myself again, has he survived? Did he inherit stamina from the ancient kings, priests, and farmers of Central America? Even after centuries of conquest, the Mayan people have survived. And Ildefonso had survived.

Back in the bungalow we faced each other once more. I signed "tree." He signed it after me. With sudden inspiration, I jumped out of my chair, found a piece of paper, and laid it in front of him. I signed "tree," mimed drawing, and gave him an encouraging nod. He signed "tree," mimed drawing with his pencil on the paper, gave me an encouraging nod, and put his pencil down. I signed "tree," again. When he once more copied me, I lost patience and signed, "No, watch me." I signed/mimed a leaf falling from the tree, which I picked up and offered to him. He repeated my moves. Frustrated, I didn't risk a third try.

Elena had mentioned numbers. I took the paper and wrote: *1 2 3*. I could find only two pennies, so I fingerspelled J-u-a-n-i-t-a across the room to a fluent signer who was looking my way, and asked her to get Juanita's attention. Juanita sprang to attention and immediately gave me the penny I somehow knew she would have. I counted each penny by pulling it toward me an inch and pointing to the corresponding number. I also counted "one, two, three," with my other hand. Then I pushed paper, numbers, and pennies across the table. "Your turn," I said out loud, gesturing an invitation to action. He counted the pennies with one hand and signed "one, two, three" with the other! He looked as if he knew what he was doing and was interested not in pleasing me but for himself. We both smiled and spent the remaining hour counting coins, writing numbers, and counting on our fingers. Ildefonso became animated, even excited, and mastered one through nine with no problems except sloppy writing and mixing up six and nine.

It was only 12:30, but I was exhausted. As I boarded the number 3 bus for home, I yawned again and again and decided not to look for a full-time job that day as I had planned. For teaching in Elena's class and interpreting, I received $4.20 an hour for less than twenty hours a week. The cost of living in Santa Monica was high, and medical-school books and equipment were outrageously priced. It looked as if my time with Ildefonso would be limited. Soon I would be forced to get a job that would pay the bills.

Hours later, over plates of spaghetti, John and I discussed Ildefonso. John had spent all day with a cadaver and was excited about the study of a live person. Since he planned to take up psychiatry, he was especially curious about Ildefonso's apparently good mental health, manifested by his continuing interest in others and attempts to interact. We were both incredulous; Ildefonso was sane after twenty-seven years of a mental isolation worse than any solitary confinement in prison. His cell had open windows: he could experience everything in the world—touch it, feel it, taste it, watch it—but only in total isolation.

No one had ever agreed or disagreed with him, mirrored, confirmed, or argued with his impressions. He had only his own mind to connect experiences, find patterns, imagine meanings, and fit together semantic puzzles. Even with shared meaning, feedback, and help in interpreting the world, many people have trouble with reality. How does one stay sane when all interpretation is generated by one's self alone?

Bob, Mary Ann, and Tom hadn't. Tom had withdrawn completely. The other two had learned to copy or simulate communication, but they couldn't make the necessary semantic connections to understand the world. Only Ildefonso appeared to be sane, interested, and curious. Could he somehow sense that there was sense? Could he perceive without words or signs what normal people receive from the language of their mothers, fathers, and friends?

The next day when I entered Room 6, Ildefonso seemed less fearful as I greeted him. Our success with the arithmetic lesson had encouraged both of us. Now he carefully unfolded a crumpled paper covered with numbers. He had practiced smoothing out his shaky lines and distinguishing a six from a nine. Why, I wondered, did numbers carry meaning for him when signs elicited only mimicry or withdrawal into fear and confusion? Was counting more intuitive and basic than naming? I pictured Adam counting and grouping animals for months before he named them.

To rest from the fatigue of our eye-to-eye search for an entrance into each other's head, we sat shoulder to shoulder, lining up numerals in progressively neater rows. I drew an addition sign between two *1*s and placed a *2* underneath. I wrote *1 + 1 + 1* with a *3* under it, then four *1*s, and so on. I explained addition by placing the corresponding number of crayons next to each numeral. He became very animated, and I introduced him to an equal sign to complete the equations. Three minutes later the crayons were unnecessary. He had gotten it. I presented him with a page of addition problems, and he was as happy as my nephew with a new dinosaur book.

While Ildefonso was playing with his nine new friends, I worked with Mary Ann. Her nutmeg eyes watched me from behind her fishbowl lenses. Excited by my attention, she grabbed a preschool workbook and opened it to simple words and colored pictures. With great deliberation she fingerspelled g-, waved her hand and shook her head, meaning "whoops," then tried again: h-o-u-s-a, another wave of hand and shake of head, -e. Her head and hand bobbed in rhythm with each letter as if stamping the word permanently in the air.

"Good," I signed, and gave her the sign for house.

She looked confused.

"H-o-u-s-e," I fingerspelled slowly; "house," I signed, then pointed to the picture beside the word *house* in her book. She pointed to the picture and began to mouth nonsense and make gestures almost identical to those of the previous day.

I paged through her book, wondering how to start again. Someone had clearly taught her fingerspelling, but did it *mean* anything to her? Unlike Ildefonso, who repeated everything without comprehension—a visual echolalia—Mary Ann simulated communication with meaningless speech and gestures. She didn't seem perturbed by the lack of meaning as long as she was acting like other people. I never saw her use language, but her communication was not all nonsense. The day before she had signed "blood" and graphically portrayed sexual intercourse via gestures. There were bits of meaning without any coherence—a string of items flung out randomly. Perhaps I could explore the intelligible items and begin to add structure.

Closing the book, I put it in front of her and signed "book." She began her lip exercises. "Book," I repeated.

"Book," she signed.

"Table." I outlined the table with my hands and bounced my flat palms on it, then repeated, "table."

"Table," she signed.

I pointed to the book, raised my eyebrows, and tilted my head toward her, mime for "What's that?"

"Book," she signed immediately.

Maybe I simply needed to get her attention. I risked a new rung. "Book yellow" (in ASL, as in Romance languages, adjectives follow nouns).

"Yellow," she signed, frowning.

"Yellow," I signed again, pointing to a yellow sun in her picture book. "Yellow," I repeated, and pointed to the flowers on her blouse.

"Yellow?" she signed with a question face, and found a yellow raincoat on the page.

"Yes, yellow," I signed encouragingly, although I had the impression this was old hat for her. I taught or reviewed several other colors, and each time she understood. When we got to red she grew agitated, and began her strange speaking and incoherent gesturing before starting her tale of blood and sex again.

I interrupted her after another "blood."

"Where?" I gestured. She pointed below her waist, described sexual intercourse, and indicated her pelvic area. "Now? Blood? Now?" I asked.

In answer she grabbed my hand and held my ring finger, signing "Man? You?" and holding up her wedding ring: "Man me."

To my relief, it was break time. I could only guess at the significance of her communication. She might have been suffering from a physical problem relating to intercourse, but she showed no sign of discomfort or pain, and her few signs and mime did not provide context.

While I searched for meanings in her gestures, she looked thoroughly content. She had never known communication without vagueness and guessing, so she apparently expected senselessness and was happy simply to interact. She could perform with signs for an exercise, but I sensed an inability to imagine signs as permanent tools. The next day the same signs might mean something different or nothing at all, like all those mouth movements she saw every day.

I wandered to the middle of the lawn feeling defeated. Either I lacked tools or these languageless minds were truly inaccessible. What appeared to be craziness— Bob's broken-record introduction, Tom's autism, Mary Ann's obsession, and Ildefonso's copying—were reasonable responses to lives that provided no reasons or explanations. Could any of them be freed from their isolation?

When I returned to Ildefonso, I struck out with the

third "tree" lesson. Pointing to and naming objects failed to communicate anything. I led, he followed. I pointed, he pointed. I signed, he signed. We had perfect rhythm, but no music. What to do? A sign popped into my head: two chirping birds looking up to a face full of perplexity, which literally translated is: ?do?do?do?do?do?do?do?

I reached for his workbook, hoping that pictures might convey what my miming did not. I found the page with C-A-T and the penciled line to the picture. It was just possible that Ildefonso's unconscious might have carried an association between the meaningless C-A-T and the picture. Desperately, I pointed to the picture. His callused fingertip landed on the cat's head. Still pointing with one hand to the picture, I signed "cat" with my other hand. He dutifully copied me and signed a sloppy "cat." I smiled and nodded my head up and down to show my pleasure. He looked satisfied or perhaps relieved as his broad hands again disappeared into the crooks of his arms.

I repeated the "cat" sign, and he repeated his inaccurate version. I brought my hand from my face (the sign is formed as if brushing whiskers onto one's cheek) and showed him the handshape. He copied me. I took his hand and uncurled all but his index finger, which remained on his thumb. Then I signed again. He repeated the sign with the right shape this time. I applauded with head nods and smiles, again pointing to the picture while signing "cat." He visually echoed everything I did, in the same way a four-year-old tries to obey incomprehensible orders that will make Mama happy. I'm sure that for him the written "cat" did not carry a clue as to what the sign meant, but I believed that this mechanical association might be his only steppingstone to the universe of symbols.

The conscious mind is always limited and struggles to assimilate, accommodate, associate, and remember. The unconscious mind, on the other hand, with apparently unlimited capacity, has no trouble at all with millions of associations and connections. I read once that the human brain is unique in the primate family not because it is so much bigger or has developed such specialized parts, but because it has such a vast connection system—countless circuits and interchanges. My hope was that Ildefonso's unconscious connections between the sign "cat," the word *cat,* the cat picture, and a real cat might begin associations that would eventually surface.

Believing that at some level we had one sign in common, I began a new mime lesson. I pretended to see a cat. I signed "cat" and coaxed the invisible creature to approach, picked it up, stroked it, and held it in one arm as I signed "cat" again with the other.

Ildefonso imitated whatever he could and never stopped to watch me. Suddenly my back and neck ached with frustration as I placed Ildefonso's hands once again on the table. They rose immediately when I started my imaginary cat routine. We were an interlocked duo. My attempts at communication turned the crank, and his hands jumped, popping up on cue like the head of a jack-in-the-box who forever hears the same nonsensical tune and springs up, smiling and oblivious.

The scraping of chairs on linoleum and rising bodies signaled the start of the morning break. I smelled the coffee from three buildings away and quickly took leave of Ildefonso. We were both exhausted from trying to figure out the other. The break was all too brief. Obsessed, I couldn't restrain myself from trying again. And again. I called my imaginary cat to my lap and petted it before signing "cat." Ildefonso called the cat to his lap and signed "cat." I hid the invisible cat behind my back and asked where it was with mime. Ildefonso did the same.

For four days, face to face, we failed to connect. My dependency on names blocked my view into his mind of no names. His survival strategy of mimicry kept him from listening—that is, paying attention to a conversation. Was it too late for him to learn language? Was I simply adding more confusion and frustration to his life?

The weekend provided a rest from these doubts, and I returned on Monday, determined to try again. It was the fifth working day since our meeting. He looked interested in everything I did, and I believed he was trying to communicate. So I kept trying too.

Cat sign, *cat,* cat picture, and imaginary cat danced together in various partnerships. I stayed with the same lesson, variation after variation. Still he insisted on copying everything I did. He didn't know how to receive. He could act and react, but he couldn't get the idea of conversing without doing. I wanted to scream at him: "I don't want you to *do* anything!"

I decided to ignore him. It was his searching eyes that had first attracted my attention; I must trust them to watch and study me. So I began the cat lesson again, but this time I had no eye contact with him. I looked instead at an imaginary student and taught him the cat connections.

I stood at the blackboard facing an empty chair, signed "cat," and wrote *cat.* I petted an imaginary cat and read the word *cat* on the board. Sitting down in the chair, I became an imaginary Ildefonso. I studied the word and frowned. Then I tilted my head back, opened my mouth slightly, and nodded as if to say, "Oh, I get it. That's a cat." As Ildefonso, I went to the board and started petting the word *cat*. Of course, the chalk streaked. I looked bewildered. What happened? Wasn't that a cat? I turned back to the teacher position and explained via mime that *cat* is not a real cat but puts the idea of cat in my head. After pointing to *cat,* I mimed taking something out of my head and putting it in the invisible Ildefonso's head. Becoming Ildefonso again, I looked thoughtful while I pointed to the word, pointed to my head, held and stroked an imaginary cat, then pointed to my head again.

I carefully avoided meeting Ildefonso's eyes, but I knew he was watching. My peripheral vision showed me that his arms were folded and not echoing my movements. I repeated the teacher-student act over and over, varying it as much as possible without losing the main idea of *cat* or "cat" triggering a picture in the brain. The *cat* on the board was written, rubbed out, and rewritten until my fingers were white.

When it was time to go, Ildefonso stared at me. I stared back and sat down. While everyone else shuffled out the door, we sat looking at each other. I rose and nodded a farewell. He sat and stared at the space I had just occupied. For the first time, I had the feeling that he wouldn't show up the next day.

On Tuesday, I was truly surprised to find him sitting in his usual corner seat. I nodded hello and opened his book to the cat picture. I pointed and posed with a "what?" on my face. Ildefonso imitated the question and pointed to the picture. Already tired, I returned to what seemed to be our only hope—the imaginary Ildefonso skit. I set up the empty chair, headed for the blackboard, and repeated the previous day's lesson. Time passed. I looked at Ildefonso. He straightened up in his chair and looked back. I went to the board, wondering if any new variation were possible. I tried a slow-motion version. At the next attempt, I looked the same, but in my head I had a Texas accent. I began to worry about my sanity. Fortunately, it was time for our fifteen-minute break.

As soon as it was over, Ildefonso returned to his seat and I to my stage. "One more time," I told myself. While I was correcting the imaginary Ildefonso, the real Ildefonso shifted in his chair. I stopped.

Suddenly he sat up, straight and rigid, his head back and his chin pointing forward. The whites of his eyes expanded as if in terror. He looked like a wild horse pulling back, testing every muscle before making a powerful lunge over a canyon's edge. My body and arms froze in the mime-and-sign dance that I had played over and over for an eternity. I stood motionless in front of the streaked *cat,* petted beyond recognition for the fiftieth time, and I witnessed Ildefonso's emancipation.

He broke through. He understood. He had forded the same river Helen Keller did at the water pump when she suddenly connected the water rushing over her hand with the word spelled into it. Yes, w-a-t-e-r and c-a-t *mean* something. And the cat-meaning in one head can join the cat-meaning in another's head just by tossing out a *cat.*

Ildefonso's face opened in excitement as he slowly pondered this revelation. His head turned to his left and very gradually back to his right. Slowly at first, then hungrily, he took in everything as though he had never seen anything before: the door, the bulletin board, the chairs, tables, students, the clock, the green blackboard, and me.

He slapped both hands flat on the table and looked up at me, demanding a response. "Table," I signed. He slapped his book. "Book," I replied. My face was wet with tears, but I obediently followed his pointing fingers and hands, signing: "door," "clock," "chair." But as suddenly as he had asked for names, he turned pale, collapsed, and wept. Folding his arms like a cradle on the table, he lay down his head. My fingers were white as I clutched the metal rim of the table, which squeaked under his grief more loudly than his sobbing.

He had entered the universe of humanity, discovered the communion of minds. He now knew that he and a cat and the table all had names, and the fruit of his knowledge had opened his eyes to evil. He could see the prison where he had existed alone, shut out of the human race for twenty-seven years.

Welcome to my world, Ildefonso, I thought to myself. Let me show you all the miracles accomplished with symbols, all the bonds and ties between human beings, young and old, and even with those dead for centuries. Come, Ildefonso, eat my "cat" and taste the sweetness of human connections. I will show you how to bathe in the swirling, magical river called Language. You can swim anywhere, meet anyone and anything, or just float on one of those lovely names. Let me open the door to this world that refused to let you join. Let me introduce you to your captors who kept you locked in a black hell of meaninglessness and incomprehensible loneliness.

3

CHAPTER

■ ■ ■

RIDING HOME ON THE NUMBER 3 BUS, everything seemed unreal. People acted as if nothing had happened. I felt the streets should have been full of cheering crowds. An innocent man had just been released from a life of imprisonment. Back in the apartment, I waited anxiously for John to come home so I could shout out my news: Ildefonso had escaped. He was no longer alone.

John arrived exhausted and weighed down with ten-pound medical books. "He did it!" I cried. "Ildefonso understood today. He realized language." John, now prone on the couch, was happy that I was happy, but too tired to appreciate the significance of the achievement.

I was suddenly impatient to see Ildefonso. I realized that he had been my most constant human contact since I moved. I was obsessed with the challenge of reaching him, discovering his wordless, signless thoughts. That day he had grasped the rope I had been throwing him. The bridge was built, the connection made. Now we could cross the chasm and face each other, sharing our new gift of conversation.

On Wednesday, in the cool morning air, I almost

skipped from the bus to the bungalow, but I hesitated once inside the door. I was expecting to see some physical difference. Instead, I found a timid Ildefonso, arms rigidly locked. I signed "Good morning," and, of course, he had no idea what I was saying.

But when I sat down across from him, he slowly nodded his head and leaned forward, his black eyes eager. For the last week he had always sat erect, observing me with keen interest but from a distance, as an outsider. Today, he lowered his head slightly as he bent over the table, shoulders forward. His look seemed to say, "We have a secret, don't we?" He moved even closer, breathing deeply. "Is it true, or did I dream this strange idea?" his dark eyes asked.

My face beamed as I signed "cat" and opened the book to the cat picture.

"Cat" he signed, but without a change of expression. I waited, but he did nothing.

"Ildefonso," I signed, his namesign which I had picked up from the teacher. Elena had probably invented it. I pointed to him.

He pointed to himself, "Me?"

"You—Ildefonso," I repeated, head nodding.

"Ildefonso," he signed looking at the wall behind me. Twenty-seven years without a name. I wondered if it meant anything to him now.

"Me—Susan," I signed, and smiled. He repeated it mechanically.

Before I had time to worry about his lack of enthusiasm, I saw Juanita waving her arm at me impatiently. The instant our eyes met, Juanita fired signs at me; she wanted to learn English, "now." "Just a minute," I answered. I set Ildefonso up with his good friends: numbers one through nine. How could I refuse? A room full of deaf people who had waited hours and days, even years, for tutoring or counseling or support from eyes that could read their hands. Ildefonso was only one of many. I could not justify spending all of my time with one student.

"Yes, Juanita, coming." Hurriedly, I wrote out some simple addition problems for Ildefonso.

Juanita demanded a lecture on English verbs: When does one use a verb with *-ing,* when not. She was sharp and quick as a magician. Her only problem was the world's slowness. I imagined her as a deaf baby figuring out that she might be missing something and pestering her parents to teach her everything, including how to hear. As I saw Juanita practice English sentences, ask for clarification, insist on explanations for rules, I thought of all the timid deaf people I had met who had been taught not to ask for anything, to stay in the background, to accept an inferior position. I wished Juanita could be cloned.

I hurried back to Ildefonso. His addition was perfect, but his numerals were crooked and full of kinks. Each was a different size. The pencil stuttered every few millimeters, waiting for the worried student to stop studying the example and return to his paper. LuAnn interrupted to ask me to work with Mary Ann, who wanted attention. I had only just returned to Ildefonso. This man had waited so long. I wanted to shout: "Stop, stop, this man needs language. Stop, we need to celebrate his first word. Stop!" How could I explain to LuAnn what had happened? LuAnn seemed annoyed by the time I spent with Ildefonso. She herself chose to keep busy wandering from student to student. Explanations were useless, and we had already been interrupted. I went to check on Mary Ann.

"Yellow," she signed as I approached, as if yellow meant hello to me, a personal greeting, our connection. We talked about colors for a while, "Book green, blouse blue." I carefully avoided "red." She animatedly simulated speech and signing, but made no sense. I realized that she needed human contact, even if nonsense was the only communication. People with language often do the same, talking about nothing. The need for attention, for spending time with someone else, outweighs the importance of intelligent content.

Leaving a more content Mary Ann, I rejoined Ildefonso. Pointing to the teacher, I signed, "Elena." He repeated the sign. His stunted movements formed quiet signs, not full or complete signs, but something like the half signs of a deaf person talking to himself. He leaned forward when his hand pointed and his eyes questioned, but his face was hard. He repeated Elena's namesign and gave an almost imperceptible nod, which I could not interpret.

I had run back from Mary Ann hoping to express my excitement over his new knowledge of personal names, especially his own new name. His dwarfed signs and self-absorption checked me. I was somehow frightened of this somber, stiff man as I watched his mechanical repetitions. He couldn't see me, he was looking into some private corner.

How was I to build on the previous day's breakthrough? What did Ildefonso's experience mean? I was no longer sure. What did he understand exactly? What should I do next?

"Susan name I/me (pointing). Susan. Ildefonso name you. Ildefonso," I signed, unthinkingly.

Elena called me from around the divider—the

teacher next door needed an interpreter. As I walked out, I looked behind me. Ildefonso had merged with the chair again.

After interpreting for a cooking class in Independent Living Skills, another way station for the lost and found, I rushed back to Room 6. Only ten minutes of Ildefonso's class remained. I started once more, but without confidence: "Name you Ildefonso; name me Susan; name she Elena. Name you?" I asked with my palms up. No response.

Yesterday's tears and Ildefonso's heaving shoulders came back to me. His reaction to names and to our world of names contained more grief than joy. And the joy had come with not the discovery of language, but merely of names. Actually, not even names, only the idea of the existence of names. How foolish I was that morning. Of course we couldn't converse. My fantasy had sprung from the knowledge of what is possible with language, which we still didn't share. My hopes receded.

On the second day after Ildefonso's revelation, I began again. "Ildefonso," I signed with a smile and sat down.

"Ildefonso," he signed.

"Good. Yes, name you Ildefonso, name me Susan." This was the ninth morning I had spent with him, and there I sat teaching him the "Me Jane, you Tarzan" introduction I had dismissed the week before.

Bending over the table, Ildefonso looked like a cat studying a spider but not yet ready to pounce. He waited until only inches divided us, ready to share some secret, but his only message was a quick bounce of his eyebrows.

"Name you?" I began.

"Name?" he defensively copied. He didn't understand the new sign. He had only just learned that names existed, and now I was asking him to understand the name for names. I realized my mistake and shelved that sign.

"Ildefonso you, Ildefonso—male. Susan me—female." I pointed to each man in the room: He—male, he—male, he—male, and then to each woman with the sign for female (the generic pronoun sign is the same as pointing so it was easy for Ildefonso to understand).

"Ildefonso—what?" The gesture for *what* is open hands facing up, circling slightly, with fingers pointing out to the world. The head tilts back and the mouth opens a little. This is an almost universal request for an explanation. I've seen variations of it from expressive eastern Europeans, Parisians, Greeks, Italians, and Mexicans. Even some Anglo-Saxons bring up their hands in a similar manner after a verbal question fails.

"Me? . . . Ildefonso."

"Yes. Ildefonso. Ildefonso—male; Susan—female; he—male, Ildefonso—what?"

"Me? Me—male."

We had talked. It was a real conversation, a very little conversation, but a conversation. We had used language without mime for the first time to carry an idea. Then we reviewed the signs of the week, which Ildefonso had seen and probably understood but had never signed: "chair," "table," "book," "door," "paper," "pencil." I added "male" and "female." Ildefonso seemed to assimilate the gender signs more easily than the names Susan, Ildefonso, and Elena. They fit his new list better.

He mimed something I didn't understand. When I gestured, shook my head, frowned, and raised my shoulders—a visual "huh?"—he pretended to write by moving

51

his pencil back and forth above the paper. Then he gestured as if signing. His eyes opened wide, his eyebrows
arched up, and he glanced quickly from his hands to the
imaginary writing. He repeated the last bit, shrugged his
shoulders, and threw up his hands, which I interpreted
as "What's this all about?" I didn't understand what he
wanted so I repeated my "huh," attempting to show
enough interest to encourage him to try again. He simulated signs again, bent over the paper, and scribbled
some marks. He looked at where he had signed, held the
paper, studied the marks, looked back at the sign space,
then at me with an inquisitive face. He was obviously
comparing signs and words, but I didn't know what he
was asking. Asking about the relationship between signs
and words seemed too abstract for someone who knew
only one word and less than a dozen signs. What explanation did he want?

I tried to clarify his comparison by writing *cat* on my
left, shifting to the right and signing "cat." He nodded,
took the paper, signed "cat," pointed to *cat,* pointed to
the door, and half-signed "door," pointed to the table and
described it with his own invented sign, and returned to
the paper, guiding his pencil down an imaginary column
under *cat.* He wanted the words. A deaf person asking
for words instead of signs. He wanted me to teach him
the written names first, the symbols that represented
sounds he could not hear.

To make sure, I signed "cat," then mimed writing
while addressing him with a questioning look. He nodded
his head. *Cat* he recognized by the general shape or,
perhaps, by one feature that he had picked out. He knew
nothing of the alphabet or that letters represented sounds.

I hesitated. Such explanations would be pointless, but I could show him words. He had waited twenty-seven years for language. He deserved to be allowed to direct his own learning. I began to give him the words he wanted.

I wrote a bigger and clearer *cat* and handed him the paper. He lowered his head and studied its form, clenched his jaw, leaning rigidly forward and uncrossing his ankles so he could set his feet flat on the floor. He was preparing for this new work like a sprinter at the starting line. He tried to copy *cat,* but the resulting scrawl was illegible. I walked behind him to guide his hand for a second *cat.* His hand, a fisted knot gripping the pencil, felt like a rock. Indeed, the lead broke when he pressed the paper for the stem of the *a.* Without looking up, he accepted another pencil and continued.

I touched his shoulder to get his attention, but he did not feel it. He was possessed by the written word. He had probably realized before that words had meaning, but he could never break the code. Perhaps he associated the unintelligible shape on a road sign with the specific reactions of drivers on the road. He must have noticed the sudden responses of a person to squiggles on a note or letter. Such a riddle for him: how could those marks trigger laughter or tears or anger? All of his life, he had seen those mysterious lines incite people to pick up telephones, crumple paper, nod, or shake their heads. Was he now remembering his life's questions about words? I would have dearly loved to pry open his skull and peer into the storm of thoughts that held him captive.

"Names, more names," he ordered by slapping the table, pointing to the door, and handing me the paper. I added to the column. Ildefonso pointed to me, to himself, to Elena; he wanted our names. S-U-S-A-N, I spelled out in big block letters. He stared at the name, attempting to smoke out the secret formula for deciphering the code. How was *cat* different from *table,* different from *Susan?* He looked up suddenly. "Susan?" he signed with his left hand while his right index finger descended on *Susan.* "Yes, Susan." *Elena,* I wrote, and he studied it.

Suddenly class was over, chairs slid back, students rose to full height and passed us, but Ildefonso studied the names, oblivious. "Me?" he asked. I-L-D-E-F-O-N-S-O, I added. His eyes widened, and he repeated his question: "Me?" "Yes, Ildefonso," I signed, and pointed to the word. His name was longer than any other word. Since he could note only general shapes, he could attach importance only to the more obvious differences, such as length. Something disturbed him about his written name, and he returned to mine. "Susan," he signed to himself, staring at the name. He didn't know any individual letter or that they could be translated to speech. He knew or sensed only the power in names and words. They held the key to understanding his life, the strange behaviors around him, and the world. He couldn't comprehend their meaning or grasp what they were any more than I could grasp $E = mc^2$, but we both knew these symbols influenced and even controlled our lives. He carefully, ceremoniously, folded the paper and placed it in his back pocket as carefully as if it were a hundred dollar bill. His farewell nod to me was almost trancelike.

Friday morning I arrived early, but Ildefonso was already there and had carefully extracted the crumpled paper from his jeans' back pocket and smoothed it out on the table. Pencil in hand, he asked for words, all the words. He wanted me to spell out the word that corresponded to each of the things around him and to the signs he had learned. I took his paper and saw that he had tried to copy the shapes of each word. I added more words. The list grew. I was anxious to teach him more than names, but I didn't want to discourage him with news about rules. Grammar could wait until he was less mesmerized by names. We practiced writing letters and words until the break.

When we got back, Ildefonso mimed a question—something about his skin and words. Although he repeated it and changed the gestures, I still didn't understand what he was asking. He tried a third time. He pointed out all of the brown-skinned people in the room, pointed to himself, mimed infants or young children eating and sleeping together, then pointed to the words while wearing a question on his face. I guessed at the question, but couldn't believe he was capable of asking what I was thinking: "Are these the words my family uses?" He could not distinguish one letter from another. All words, English or otherwise, looked foreign to him, except *cat*. What possible clue did he have that more than one set of names existed?

Parallel to the column of English words, I wrote the Spanish equivalents: *table—mesa, chair—silla,* and so on. With my finger, I followed the English column down the page, pointed to myself and my skin and referred back to the English. Next, I followed the Spanish column, pointed to Ildefonso and the other Mexicans in the room and to his skin. He held the paper halfway between the table and his face, examining the two lists.

"Table?" he asked, pointing to *table,* then to my skin. "Table?" he repeated, pointing to *mesa* and his skin.

"Yes," I answered reluctantly, sensing his rising frustration. He was silent for what seemed like a long time before asking for the rest of the Spanish words. I added one or two more and shrugged my shoulders, pointing to a couple of blank lines to indicate my ignorance of those Spanish words. He was surprised and pointed to the blank spaces, asking, "Really?" with his face and posture. I shrugged my shoulders again and nodded my head. He lost himself in the two lists for a while, then put the wrinkled paper on the table and began to copy the words.

I watched and, as always, wondered what was in his mind. How had he come up with the idea of two languages when he still didn't know one? (Later, someone pointed out to me that he probably had showed his uncle the list of English words, and his uncle hadn't understood them.) His writing stopped, but his hand still gripped the pencil and he stayed bent over the paper. I touched the back of his left hand, which was lying near the center of the table. With a sudden sigh, he collapsed onto the paper and, as before, sobbed silently with his head cradled in the crook of his arm. The table rocked with his grief. It was too much: in less than a week he had learned about ASL, English, and Spanish names. How could he imagine or accept more than one language when the notion of any language was a vague new dream? His question had been like a stone thrown innocently at a mountain, triggering an avalanche too heavy for him to bear.

What had I done? Had I brought Ildefonso to the edge of language where he had a view of his tragedy, a knowledge of his disease, but no hope of relief or a cure? Was it too late for him to join this world of names, where one must learn one set for talking to white people and another for talking to brown? He had to learn not only

names, but which were the right ones to use with the
people he loved. Ildefonso was in the company of poets,
I realized, recalling lines from "The Rising of the Sun"
and "Lauda" by Czeslaw Milosz:

> Everything would be fine if language did not
>   deceive us by finding
> different names for the same thing in different
>   times and places . . .
> A word should be contained in every single
>   thing
> But it is not.
>
> That a meaning would not flare in the long
>   and wakeful night
> Gave me grief, and then despair,
> But the words would yield no light.

My hand rested on Ildefonso's shoulder for a long moment—my farewell. I left, once again wondering if I could
return on Monday, if Ildefonso would return.

4

CHAPTER

■ ■ ■

IN TEN DAYS, ILDEFONSO HAD TRIED to vault over the wall that had separated him from the rest of the world for almost three decades. But despite his first running start, he remained outside of language. I began to wonder if it were possible for an adult to travel from language-lessness to all the rules for manipulating symbols and the complicated structures of language. Were we both deluding ourselves? Perhaps I had simply opened the door far enough for me to join him in his prison where we both were trapped.

That Friday night, Ildefonso's crying haunted me. If it was too late to learn language, I had only tortured him by offering the unobtainable. My efforts had robbed him of his only cushion—ignorance. I thought of Charlie, the retarded man in *Flowers for Algernon,* and the experiment to make him intelligent. In the end, when Charlie regressed to his original state, he had gained only the awareness that he was different and dumb. Was I helping Ildefonso toward language, or setting him up in an experiment of frustration?

During the weekend I looked for help. Someone

must have taught language to an adult before. I called Laura, the coordinator of interpreters at the registry that hired me. She knew everyone local in the field of deafness. She referred me to an adult-education teacher who had had years of experience teaching deaf adults. I called the teacher and found she had never taught prelingual adults. She referred me to a Mr. Karpf, who specialized in late language acquisition in deaf children. I called Mr. Karpf, who told me stories about multihandicapped and developmentally disabled deaf children who had learned language late in life. The oldest child that he had taught was eleven. He had never heard of anyone teaching an adult a first language, but he thought Mrs. Johnson down in Orange County might know of someone. Mrs. Johnson told me more good stories, some once or twice removed: "So and so told me about someone who did such and such." Mrs. Johnson suggested the state mental hospital. She had heard they did something with sign language and catatonic patients. Perhaps they could answer my questions. I didn't think so and ignored the suggestion.

I called Laura back to see if she had another lead. She suddenly remembered Ursula Bellugi. Everyone who learns sign language hears about all the great interpreters, song-signers, deaf actors, and the linguist Ursula Bellugi. Since sign language was not perceived as equal to other languages until recently, the study of it differs from that of any other second language. When one studies German, for example, one doesn't learn about Martin Luther translating the Bible and standardizing the German language or about the most eloquent poets in modern Germany before learning how to conjugate a few irregular verbs. Sign students, however, before they learn the most basic conversational fluency, hear stories of the history of ASL, the names of favorite dramatic signers and top interpreters, many myths and truths surrounding deafness and signs—and about Ursula Bellugi.

Ursula Bellugi is a linguist at the Salk Institute in La Jolla where, among other things, the biological foundations of language are studied. Belugi studies American Sign Language, working with signers and children of signers. Her background is in language acquisition. Once I heard her name suggested, I was confident she would have the references and the information I needed. I called her secretary and arranged an appointment. Until then I would have to continue alone.

On Monday morning, both Ildefonso and I showed up. He accepted my beginning sign lesson without protest. Words, we both agreed silently, would have to wait. Ildefonso responded mechanically. He initiated nothing. After reviewing the few names we had in common, I decided an arithmetic lesson would soothe us.

Ildefonso could add and subtract using numerals one through nine; he was ready for ten. Could I teach more complicated arithmetic without language? Even with language, I didn't know how to teach ten. It was so automatic to me, I had forgotten how I learned it. I drew nine lines and then, after a pause, added a tenth line and drew a circle around the set. I wrote *10* above the whole circle. Ildefonso stared at it vacantly. Then I remembered being five in a one-room school house in Wyoming. The teacher showed me a bundle of crayons and a single crayon above two *1*s on my paper. I counted nine crayons in front of Ildefonso, added one, tied the bundle with a rubber band

and placed it on a piece of paper. Below it I wrote *1 0*. Then I wrote *1* through *10* and pointed to the bundle for ten. I continued with *11, 12, 13, 14, 15,* adding crayons. I repeated the lesson. As long as Ildefonso watched the crayons and paper, I kept repeating. I made two bundles and placed them together, writing *2 0* below them. Slowly, I wrote *1* through *20* and placed the corresponding crayons above each numeral. Ildefonso studied what I had written—and got it without any more help. He found the symbols for numbers easy compared to signs or words. Apparently, arithmetic already resided in his brain.

He and I went to lunch together, and I threw names—milk, coffee, sandwich—at him. He responded with feeble copies, all the while looking elsewhere. Then we sat in silence. He ate and studied the signers and talkers in the orange lounge. When he finished eating, he folded his arms and looked exactly as he had when I first met him. What did he understand? Did he think of language as simply a more permanent string of names than his gestures, or did he somehow glimpse a more sophisticated system?

On the bus ride home, I became convinced that we could never truly meet. His questions and my questions would never find answers. He would always wonder how to break the code and find meaning and rules. I would always wonder what had caused his tears and, especially, his trance when confronted with written names.

I missed the bus the next morning and was late. "Sorry," I signed, hoping Ildefonso might glean a little of the meaning from my apologetic manner and rapid breathing. He gave me his usual acknowledgment nod and nothing more. Using my lateness, I signed "clock" and began talking about time. Ildefonso sat and stared.

During that week, I tried several times to teach him what the numbers on a clock meant. He seemed to understand that they corresponded to an event like class or lunch break, but they could just as well have been pictures of flowers. The movement or position of the black hands meant nothing to him.

I shifted to more general notions of time: morning, evening, and the idea of a day based on the sun rising and setting. Ildefonso eventually learned the signs for sun, sunrise, sunset, but not day or night. I acted out working and eating lunch and working again, then going home, resting, and eating once more as the sun disappeared. I signed "morning," "noon," and "evening" after the appropriate mimed acts, repeated the whole thing, and signed "day," which looks like the previous signs all put together. His face was blank.

We were stuck in the present tense. I abandoned the idea of time and tried adjectives to add to his names: "Table hard, book hard, hair soft, clothes soft." Ildefonso kept trying to do something with the table or the book and looked worried that something was wrong with his hair or clothes.

After his first awareness of names, his progress became agonizingly slow. All he and I shared was the idea of language, not language itself. We had to wade through the murky vagueness of mime and temporary symbols. Ildefonso poked at new signs for hours or days, trying to figure out their shapes and uses. Sometimes he found the right niches in his brain for them, and his vocabulary grew slowly.

He signed nouns exclusively. Language still meant only names to him. Syntax, tense, or any symbol other than a noun remained unknown and unimaginable. A name that could be used with many people or written down to be understood by someone at another time and another place was magic enough for him. He wanted more and more names. I knew that names alone would never be language, but he didn't.

All my verb lessons failed. Common sense led me to start out with visual, easily understood actions like stand, sit, write. Common sense was wrong. Stand, sit, write were all orders to him when he understood their meaning, but he could not grasp them as symbols for action. Instead, he looked confused, wondering why I ordered him around senselessly.

For days I tried different action signs: see, eat, drink, read, sleep. Ildefonso never once repeated them as signs to learn and use with names, but always as an order. It took me years to figure out the obvious: he simply didn't need them. Miming action is easy, effective, and free of guesswork. Who does what to whom and when or in what sequence are often difficult to figure out, but the action itself is clear. He understood obvious visual actions immediately and even invisible actions like love, understand, and suspect when acted out with hands and faces.

I tried adjectives again. One morning I thought of colors as an introduction to descriptive words. I lined up different books and signed, "Book blue, book red, book orange, book brown, table brown, wall orange." Ildefonso looked confused when he saw two names for one item. I used the crayons, pointed to clothing and pictures and as many different things of the same color as possible.

This red, that red, that red, I repeated, until the redness became separate from what was red. After seeing colors used with many unrelated objects about eight different times, he understood. We both regained some of the enthusiasm of the previous week. Ildefonso double checked, "Book blue, table brown?"

"Yes, yes, right," I signed, smiling over the first successful communication in days. We practiced a few color signs, and I added a few more. The lesson stopped abruptly when I signed "green." Once he saw which color green referred to, he ducked down, hunched his shoulders, and mimed hiding. He fearfully looked from side to side, all the while signing "green, green." I had no idea what he was talking about.

"Green what?" I signed and gestured. He pretended to hide again and looked terrified, reacting to his "green" as if it were a snake. Many color signs move from left to right with a wriggle motion like a snake or scurrying lizard, but perhaps Ildefonso was really describing a snake. Perhaps he had had a frightening experience with one. It was my only guess, so I mimed a snake slithering toward me and tried to hide. "Green," I signed with my right hand, and turned my left arm into a snake. I looked at my two arms and then at Ildefonso. He leaned back against his chair and abandoned the subject.

The green story didn't discourage me; he understood his first adjectives. Perhaps they were easier than verbs because they distinguished one book or one shirt from another, the way names distinguished one thing from another. Using his new vocabulary, I introduced the verb *like*. After spreading three crayons out, I studied them while signing "red," "blue," and "orange." I looked at them a long time and then chose the red one, saying, "Red I like, blue okay, orange okay, but"—and I shifted my posture and body position to show a difference—"red I like." I lined up the crayons of all the colors Ildefonso could sign, listed them as I pointed to each one, and, with a sweep of my hand, asked Ildefonso to state his preference. I repeated the question after setting up different choices, but Ildefonso didn't answer.

The question of what was in his head continued to plague me. His experiences as an isolated individual must differ dramatically from those of people in communities. The more abstract the concept I introduced him to, the more I wondered about his interpretation. If, as seemed likely, no one had ever asked him for his preference, if he had never practiced asserting his likes and dislikes, how could he form "I like" in his head? Life had forced him to be passive and accept whatever came his way. Would he ever learn enough of our language and thinking to be able to tell me his thoughts and his experiences?

Finally the day of my appointment with Ursula Bellugi arrived. Now, I felt, everything would be solved. Dr. Bellugi immediately put me at ease with her casual manners and unpretentious dress, and she listened patiently while I explained my situation and my need for expert help. After asking a few questions, she gave me a list of articles and books on language acquisition. They all concerned children, she explained; she knew of no one who had studied first language acquisition in adults. There were the accounts of "wild" persons who were found from time to time, but she didn't think they would be useful to me, since children, deaf, wild, or normal, differ greatly from adults in language acquisition. The human brain changes dramatically from infancy to post-puberty, making language learning a completely different task for an adult. She apologized for not being able to offer me more and wished me luck. I left feeling helpless and alone.

The next day I faced Ildefonso, asking myself what we had accomplished. I got a little comfort from the fact that Ildefonso could add and subtract and count past twenty. He knew fewer than twenty nouns and only seven adjectives—all of them colors. He had no verbs, no tense, and never signed more than two signs in a row before he began miming and inventing gestures. These accomplishments didn't even come close to looking like language. He and I were connected by mime, raised eyebrows, and *cat*. We knew each other's names, but nothing else about each other.

Paul Austen, in *The City of Glass*, invented a languageless character who, like Ildefonso, had no name until adulthood. This fictional man tells a visitor, "I am Peter Stillman. That is not my real name. My real name is Peter Rabbit. In the winter I am Mr. White, in the summer I am Mr. Green. Strange, is it not?" I wondered if the name Ildefonso was any more real to its owner.

5

CHAPTER

■■■

"ILDEFONSO, YOU STUDENT."

"Ildefonso, me?"

"Yes, you, Ildefonso student," I repeated and mimed reading a book while frowning as if trying to figure something out. "Student (*learner*, literally) you."

"Me? Ildefonso."

"Yes. Ildefonso, you."

And that was that. Room 6 felt like a prison with its lack of windows and its wandering inmates. Yet Ildefonso and I chose to remain together sharing the same stale air. We mimed, gestured, and made faces at each other more than we signed. We misunderstood messages. We played charades for hours and guessed and guessed and guessed. Usually, I started the game by introducing a new sign, using it in four or five different mimed contexts to define it. Ildefonso raised and lowered his head slowly, either to demonstrate possible understanding or to nudge me to continue trying; I never knew which. Then Ildefonso tried. His eyebrows pushed up a wrinkle on his forehead—his question mark. I watched his gestured question over and over and attempted a guess after the fourth try, another guess after the fifth. I knew that I guessed wrong when he sat back, lowered his eyelids slightly, and crossed his arms. The next hour or the next day, we started again.

Yet he continued. Even after meaningless interactions or two hours of work for just one complete thought, he still tried. He didn't know anything about better communication, so he probably thought it was all this difficult. He preferred the hard work, even if he gleaned only a fragment of an idea, to his former isolation and meaninglessness. Bertrand Russell once wrote how even arduous means are enjoyed "if the end is ardently desired . . . A boy will toil uphill with a toboggan for the sake of a few brief moments of bliss during the descent. No one has to urge him to be industrious; however he may puff and pant he is still happy." The few moments of shared understanding gave Ildefonso enough incentive to keep him struggling uphill.

His persistence inspired me to keep trying. Even with hours of no mutual understanding, or after a day of no progress, I couldn't give up. His animation since he had gained his awareness of names communicated his desire. His more alert face, movements, and posture encouraged me. Besides, admitting defeat would be too painful. I would hate myself if I had only tantalized him with the unobtainable. Language had to be possible for him. I refused to believe that he was a hopeless case. He seemed to sense language and to reach for what he didn't understand. He now signed almost thirty signs. Granted that the signing chimps and the gorilla, Koko, have done better, these thirty signs at least proved that Ildefonso understood the idea of symbols. He must be able, I insisted to myself, to progress, to learn more signs and actually link two, then three, together.

We both refused to give up. John had managed to obtain a student loan so I could postpone job-hunting and continue working with Ildefonso. Every morning at 8 a.m., I entered Room 6 of Bungalow D, and every morning I found Ildefonso in the same chair waiting for me. For days, we mirrored each other's interested and questioning faces, *believing* communication could improve.

I no longer expected another sudden revelation. We both accepted our plodding, uphill conversations and were encouraged whenever one day seemed better than the day before. Replacing some gestures and mime with one or two signs sometimes took weeks, when it was possible at all. Baby-talk signing, two-sign sentences, began to appear among our gesturing and charades. Although Ildefonso was still an infant (Latin for *without speech*), he was a baby in language only. His baby talk carried the weight and bulk of adult content. Our dialogues were far too complicated for one- or two-sign utterances and produced more frustration than mutual understanding.

When a baby learns a new sign or word, it represents an equally new thing or experience. The experience of water barely precedes the hearing of the sound or the seeing of the sign for water. Ildefonso had no such luxury or the time a baby has to watch the world unfold. His head held twenty-seven years of sights and smells, tactile sensations and feelings, along with thousands of unexplained incidents. When he finally understood a sign or word, it often triggered questions and stories, most of which I could not decipher. Ildefonso wanted the world explained in the equivalent of "mama," "doggie," and "wazzat."

Although he now knew of something beyond languagelessness, he didn't have enough symbols to convey a complete thought. Mime and gesture could not describe how he had survived or who he was. Nor could his primitive acting and pointing ask the questions he had puzzled over all his life. From Ildefonso's perspective, however, he now possessed the great secret, the magic formula that had always eluded him, and he wanted to use it. He began to ask questions and sometimes tried desperately to tell me something, but 98 percent of the message he still mimed. With all of my concentration and imagination I could not understand more than one communication out of ten.

Though often discouraged, I kept trying to form questions to ask him about how he survived or grew up. Although he never fully comprehended them, I think he sensed my desire to learn about his life. Sometimes he tried to answer what he guessed my question to be. I never understood his answers, either because of lack of context to hold his string of gestures together or because his life was too alien to understand.

I gleaned only hints. The biggest one came with his insistence that I understand his "green" story. Every time I signed "green," he leaned forward, stared unblinkingly into my eyes, and signed "green, green." The same intense and energetically mimed story followed, peppered with "greens." Ildefonso told me that someone or something grabbed someone; then something about arms; then "green" and traveling or movement and others or the same ones who did the grabbing and "green." He repeated this story five, six, maybe a dozen times. I could never understand it. No other communication of his carried such emotion and produced as much animation as the "green" story. I inferred from his intensity and repetition that when I understood the meaning behind it I would begin to know Ildefonso.

For hours, days, weeks, and finally months, Ildefonso and I played mountain climbers. We plaited, tossed, tugged, and tested strands of meaning. Lines had to be thrown repeatedly until they were finally caught and attached. Gradually, sometimes with agonizing slowness, we tied knots, wove a pattern, and added breadth, height, and thickness to our rickety bridge. Slowly, as imperceptibly as a tree grows, we communicated.

"Ildefonso—student, him, him, her (pointing) student, student, student," I tried again, using the successful male/female lesson as a model. "Susan—teacher, Elena—teacher, LuAnn—teacher," I continued with mimed descriptions. The sign "student" is made by one hand scooping up something from the other hand and pressing it in the forehead, conveying the idea of transferring knowledge from a book to the brain.

"Me?" Ildefonso asked, and acted out a confused inquisitive person, pointing to the paper, then to someone signing, then turning back to me with his hands out for an explanation. He mimed gesturing and pseudo-signing, ending with his gesture for *explain this?* "Me?" he signed again and looked at my hands to see the new sign.

"Student you," I replied.

"Me, Ildefonso, student. Teacher you." He got it.

"Yes. Good," I signed.

While he was practicing his new names, I saw the opportunity for teaching verbs. The signs "teacher" and "student" contain the verbs *to teach* and *to learn*. First, we worked on writing letters. Ildefonso practiced handwriting and distinguishing between similar looking letters. He looked happy when he wrote. In spite of his crisis over words, he occasionally asked for the translation of a sign and carefully added the new word to his list, the same now-tattered piece of paper he had begun with. He carried it, like a precious document, neatly folded in his back pocket. I used the writing lesson to explain that I "teach" letters and he "learns" letters. After a few variations on that theme, Ildefonso used his first verb signs, teach and learn: The verbs that finally registered as verbs, that is, as permanent symbols for specific actions, were ones that couldn't easily be mimed. They were signs he needed.

I wondered if he would use them again on his own. He continued to react to verb lessons as orders, and when he did seem to understand, to add a verb to his vocabulary, he used it only when prompted. He never combined a verb with a noun. Verb plus noun did not seem as natural or automatic as names to him. I drilled him on verb phrases and added new verbs, always hoping to improve our exchanges of questions and answers.

Many times, I tried too hard. Once I created two giant columns in space on either side of me. In the left hand column I mimed, then signed: "see," "walk," "sit," "stand," "read," "eat," "run," and "teach." On the right I listed Ildefonso's vocabulary: "door," "table," "book," etc., and, of course, "cat." "Names, here," I signed above the now-invisible list on my right. "Activities, over here," I signed on my left side. Ildefonso suddenly looked sleepy. Instead of expressing bewilderment or lack of comprehension, he just blanked out.

I met the same poker face and sleepy eyes whenever

I attempted to teach any of our conventions concerning time. I tried more clock lessons. He yawned. I described parts of the day and practiced greetings, such as "Good morning" and "Good evening." He rubbed his eyes. The only sign he seemed to be interested in was the sign that pointed to the past. It could be translated as *before* or *a while ago* or *once upon a time*. I couldn't be sure he understood it. He never used it, but when I signed "in-the-past" and described its meaning, his eyes stayed open.

While any lesson involving time met a quick death, the study of arithmetic continued to thrive. Whenever I had to interpret or work with other students, I prepared arithmetic lessons for Ildefonso. With little difficulty he learned to multiply and with only a bit more difficulty, to divide. Even though he had used money, he had never understood the relationship between one coin and another, or one denomination and another. He quickly learned to apply his counting skills to coins and bills. He was beginning to attach meaning and rules to some of his life's experiences. In arithmetic, a teacher soon became superfluous. I hoped for his day of independence from a language teacher as well.

I had never considered being a teacher. I thought schools and educational institutions had very little to do with education. When I worked with Ildefonso, I began to realize that what he and I were doing was much more similar to what Socrates did with his companions than to what usually happens in a classroom. In a dialogue the teacher is indistinguishable from the student. My lectures to Ildefonso never fostered understanding or created new paths; our dialogues, in contrast, were never wasted experiments, even if they failed to convey the intended message. We always improved, at least a little, with each round. While gradually Ildefonso memorized vocabulary, I learned how to teach.

Ildefonso recovered from his word trauma, and his curiosity revived, surfacing in questions. His mind, quick and receptive, opened to the meanings that hid behind his new signs, and, via mime, he asked for elaboration. His mind was certainly not a *tabula rasa*; thousands of experiences and sensations had etched impressions and stimulated thinking. But his mind was empty of all information that needs language as its conduit. It didn't matter how smart he was. No one can learn history in isolation unless he is able to live in all times and places. Nor could Ildefonso know geography without traveling every mile of the world. He was still an alien. He patiently memorized vocabulary even when the meaning appeared dull, hazy, and foreign. He sensed that these building blocks could gradually construct windows from which he could finally view our world.

His open and ready mind was a teacher's paradise. I got immense gratification from the way in which it gobbled up everything given it and asked for more. Ildefonso's intellectual meals often took weeks of preparation, but our exertion only increased our mutual sense of accomplishment when he finally received a message from my world. And I couldn't help feeling flattered to be considered an expert on every subject. Ildefonso opened my eyes to the tremendous wealth of even elementary-school education. By sixth grade, I had accumulated more information and tools than many people around the globe accumulate in a lifetime.

Ildefonso was a perfect student and, as such, an enlightening teacher. His trust and innocence, however, were a teacher's hell. He deferred to me utterly. Everything I said seemed to be accepted as the entire unadulterated truth. His belief in me frightened me. If I didn't know an answer or could not explain something, he acted hurt, as if the only possible reason for not answering was that I believed he was too backward to understand. I hated that reaction, but without the tools of argument, I could not counter his implied accusation. I also hated to explain something horrible about the world, like why Anita, one of the students, was crying on Elena's shoulder after being beaten by her husband. I felt guilty by association. I imagined that Ildefonso was looking at me and demanding action, as if to say, "You have so much power; you understand situations and can affect them with the magic of words and signs. Why don't you do something? It's your world and your people. Do something." Compared to Ildefonso, I was a god. Like a Martian who befriends the first earthling he meets, Ildefonso mistook me for the leader of my planet. He couldn't know that most of my language and information was shared and common.

I worried about his reaction to all the information accompanying language, all of the black spots in humanity which ignorance had hidden from him. I remembered Caliban in *The Tempest,* who learned from Prospero about the world and how to speak. Caliban blamed his teacher for teaching him to curse. I hoped Ildefonso would neither learn to curse because of my answers, nor blame me, the bearer of bad news. In any case, he had learned so little language I had no cause to worry yet.

6

CHAPTER

■■■

DURING MANY DISCOURAGING DAYS, I wondered what kept us working. In the first few weeks of our work together, Ildefonso's progress was not great enough to encourage the student in him or the teacher in me. What pushed us every morning to face each other? It's obvious now, in retrospect. When I look back, I don't recall the student Ildefonso, but Ildefonso, my friend. As friends, we pushed each other to explore. Without understanding any specific objectives or direction, we knew we were involved in an adventure together. Our work included discovery of the self, the other, and possibilities—the stuff of all friendships. Life was re-examined and re-viewed and found new. Inner thoughts and feelings, which surface in an atmosphere of trust, create new combinations and alter perceptions. A new friendship can sometimes cause one to feel that life is happening for the first time. Ildefonso and I experienced this newness and the challenge of rethinking Everything.

Empowered by each other's interest, we could see chinks and holes in walls that had formerly seemed crack-safe and impenetrable. I could not have stretched my imagination to capture ideas for converting concepts into pictures in the air without his forehead's tense muscles and his rigid, alert posture. Ildefonso searched and studied my strange behavior until he glimpsed meaning. Without the support of his earnest black eyes, my unrehearsed mime and caveman gestures would have collapsed. I would have given up the first day. Instead, even in that short first day, I began to care for this man who lived alone, thought apart, yet reached for communication.

We began as teacher and student. Ildefonso's first vocabulary naturally related to our classroom and our initial relationship: paper, book, teacher, student. Our teacher-student relationship became secondary, however, two weeks after we met, one week after he discovered names. That morning Ildefonso surprised me with a sign I hadn't taught him. He signed, "Dumb me." Then he pointed to me and described my head as big (full). He slouched, hung his jaw, made miniature nonsense gestures, and signed, again: "Dumb me."

"No! Not (head shaking) dumb," I argued. Where did he pick up that sign? I was glad that he was learning signs on his own, but "dumb"! What a terrible first sign to share with me. I was very sorry that he learned an insult and used it against himself.

"Dumb me," he repeated, and lowered his head as if in shame.

"No, no, no!" I shouted with both hands. I tried to explain for the first time the difference between hearing and deafness. My description of sound and hearing basically showed names being absorbed into my ears, whereas his ears were stopped up. The names couldn't get through. The light in his eyes dimmed, and he folded

his arms—reliable evidence that this communication began and ended as a monologue. Even with language, some
deaf people never understand hearing. The idea to a person born deaf that meaning can be carried via sound is
ludicrous. Why did I think mime and simple gestures
could possibly convey this foreign and, to many deaf people, insane idea?

I immediately changed to another explanation:
"Baby you (over there), baby me (here)." I exaggerated
"baby," which is one of the more iconic signs—that is, a
picture sign that can convey meaning even to a nonsigner.
I put the two babies on the floor and with two flat palms
on top of the babies' heads, I slowly raised my hands and
the babies grew to be children. "This child," pointing to
one and then to myself, "this one, Susan. She went to
school, to a classroom like this one," I gestured and
mimed. My flat palm, once again on the child's head, rose
some more, showing growth. I acted out, "This child
continued to attend school. This other child—no school.
This child—you, Ildefonso. School me, no school you."
I mimed and signed, "No, dumb you; smart you, smart,"
and taught him a new sign.

Ildefonso followed my movements with interest,
which I interpreted as an indication of some understanding. He had unfolded his arms. I repeated the entire story.
This lesson was far more important than my prepared
lesson on verbs. I would pound this comparison into the
air until I convinced him of our essential equality. During
the third round, I saw an opportunity not only to see how
much he understood, but to ask my first question re-
garding his life: "This child, me—school. This (other)
child, you—what?" I was hoping he would guess the right
question and describe what he did as a child.

"Child this-high me?" Ildefonso responded.

"Yes. What's that child doing?" I mimed, by appearing to have trouble seeing the child and by describing a few activities in the context of a question.

Ildefonso extended his arm and held his cupped hand out. Then he moved his open hand back and forth in front of imaginary people. He begged. The height of the child was the height of a four- or five-year-old. While I ate three meals a day and sat every week for years in school, this boy begged. I'm sure some days he received nothing in his upturned palm, and he and his family went hungry. The verb lesson could wait.

I tried to show that the two children, Susan and Ildefonso, were equal by indicating they had the same size heads and by making their heights equal. Then I taught him the sign for "friend," one of my favorite signs. One index finger curls around the other to form this sign. The abstract idea of a bond, a link, becomes a literal link when one index finger is offered and the companion's finger accepts, curling around the first. "Ildefonso, Susan—friend," I concluded. Ildefonso and I held fingers forming "friend." I think he understood. The teacher-student roles became secondary. We were friends.

Without a human exchange, Ildefonso could never have learned language. Language is so entwined with human behavior, it is like a living organism. Some say that the advent of language replaced human evolution, became not only an integral aspect of humanness, but the most influential factor in human development. Language learning in isolation is impossible. Computers, books, and television can provide practice, explanations, a few rules or vocabulary items, but only human beings can add the ingredients that make language something more than a limited stagnant code. Even we who know language cannot learn a second language from a book alone, unless the language is no longer alive.

Two weeks after learning "friend," Ildefonso sat in his usual chair, facing away from the door, twisting his torso and turning his head so that he saw each person immediately as he or she stood in the doorway. When I opened the door and our eyes met, he turned back instantly, aligned himself in his chair, and bent over some paper as if reading. I knew he had something to tell me. He continued studying the alphabet and a few words on his paper until I sat down and faced him. He looked up at me, then to the right and left to make sure no one was watching. Ildefonso showed me his new sign. "Love-you," he signed, gently hugging his chest with the love sign. His eyes rose shyly. When I remember it now, I am ashamed of my reaction. I spent the next thirty minutes explaining the difference between "love" and "like": "Ildefonso, Susan friend. You I like." Later I realized that I've rarely had such an intense and moving friendship. I am sorry now that I was such a prude. Ildefonso had communicated his feelings about our friendship and its specialness, and I, like a schoolmarm, distanced myself from him with a lecture on "like" and "love." Many languages don't even have such a distinction.

For four months Ildefonso and I worked together, exploring language and languagelessness in each other. A bond developed, the special attachment that two people form when they survive or witness the same trauma. A unique kind of intimacy develops between them if they share a common disaster, even though one may be choosing to experience what fate brings the other. The drown-

ing swimmer and the lifeguard are indistinguishable as
they fight the riptide: both risk losing their lives. After I
decided to try communication with Ildefonso and sat facing him and his world, we became equals. My knowledge
of English and ASL was useless. We faced languagelessness together.

We sat in the same cell, stared at the same prison
walls, and worked to escape. Of course, I could have quit
and returned to language, but part of me would have
remained in prison with my friend. I chose to return to
language with the prisoner who invited me to end his
solitary confinement. Whether as parent and child, lovers,
or friends, when humans bond, separation is never possible without loss. Sharing imprisonment, war, illness, or
natural disasters exposes us to our most essential human
needs, forces us to trust one another openly and as equals.
The resulting connection, even if it is between strangers
for only a brief time, is a powerful one.

In *Prisoner Without a Name, Cell Without a Number,*
Jacobo Timmerman describes his survival of torture and
imprisonment. In the midst of inhuman—dehumaniz-
ing—treatment, Timmerman despaired, as all of us would.
He put his eye to a peephole in the door of his solitary-
confinement cell and looked out. Across the hall, framed
by another prison door, an eye looked back. It was impossible for the prisoners to tell color, age, or even gender. Without names or communication, the two
acknowledged each other's individual value and their mutual humanness. Each knew that the other understood his
suffering. Each eye projected hope, reminding the other
that we are never utterly alone.

When Ildefonso and I were tense and exhausted from

our failed transactions, we knew that we bore the frustration together. Ildefonso's alert eyes offered enough support to sustain my efforts, gesture after gesture. And nothing I did helped Ildefonso achieve language more than directing my gaze at him, hour after hour, insisting that there was something to understand.

Sometimes, though, I did feel alone. He expressed much more satisfaction than I over understanding a simple conversation that had sometimes taken hours to work out. He thought that was excellent. He thought that was language. I knew better, but I could not tell him how much better and faster thoughts could travel. Ildefonso reminded me of a baby whose curiosity draws him to a snake and who sits enchanted watching the dance of loops and curls. He doesn't know the snake can do more. He doesn't know that he can lose his life if he stays still. Someone has to shriek to save the baby. My constant insistence on Ildefonso's attention was a shout. He had to move.

The comparisons are not good. The danger he faced was not that of a drowning man or of a baby facing a snake. I was not his lifeguard or his guardian. Nor was he in any physical imprisonment. There was nothing else like his languageless life. No one could describe languagelessness except Ildefonso himself. The pictures helped me only to try to understand what happened between us, between any humans who succeed in surviving intolerable conditions. I didn't understand him or his life. I didn't know what I was doing, but thinking of languagelessness as a prison helped me. I knew I had to enter his cell, sit on the floor with him, and, from his point of view, try to see where the door to language opened. Only then could I point him in the right direction.

7

ONE DAY OUR USUAL CLASSROOM TABLE was taken, so
Ildefonso sat at a corner of a table next to the door. We
were constantly distracted by the sudden brightness outside as the door opened and by students bumping our
shoulders as they passed. We could not concentrate with
our usual intensity, and the dialogue bounced slowly between us.

Then the door swung open, and the outside glare
momentarily blinded us. After the door closed, a blurred
dark profile took on colors and features. Only inches away
stood my old friend, Cal, who had convinced me to interpret while I was looking for a full-time job. Now he
was smiling under his thick gray mustache and searching
for the next opportunity for mischief. We hugged and
signed to each other our pleasure over this unexpected
meeting.

Cal had been the professor in a course on Sociolog-
ical Aspects of Deafness that I took while I was studying
ASL at the state university in Northridge. He had a dark
Italian face and a mustache that matched his bushy white
eyebrows and hair. His face reflected boyish innocence,
until he winked. He had an amazingly seductive wink.

When I first began to study sign language and could barely say anything beyond an introduction or greeting, he patiently deciphered my clumsy signs, jerky fingerspelling, and habitual mouth movements. For months he entertained me and the rest of the class with his stories about being deaf. The last time I had seen him before moving to Los Angeles he had been in the hospital recovering from a heart attack. When I saw him again, three years later, the week before I met Ildefonso, I was overjoyed that he was still alive. He was happy that I could now sign clearly and relieved that I no longer compulsively formed words with my mouth—a habit that deaf people call "a hearing accent." He stroked his chin, touching the corners of his mustache on the upstrokes, and his eyes smiled when I used a very un-English ASL idiom. Then he had urged me to sign up as an interpreter. I explained to him that interpreting made me feel like a language machine that was plugged in to interpret and unplugged at the end of the appointment or lecture. I hardly ever got to know the deaf client, and I was often uncomfortable in interpreting situations. Although sign language interpreters follow a code of ethics based on international simultaneous vocal interpreting, sign-language interpreting is not like United Nations interpreting. In the U.N., the interpreter is simply a channel between two equal cultures and two languages of equal status. Unfortunately, deaf people and hearing people are not considered equal, and until very recently, signed languages were not even considered distinct languages. Deaf persons are usually seen as hearing people without working ears rather than as members of a linguistic minority. I explained to him that I would rather teach sign language and participate in other ways that promote better understanding of the deaf community.

Cal continued stroking his chin and nodding his head during my sermon. I told him I was looking for a job in the health field. Didn't he think it more important that signers, both deaf and hearing, become professionals in various fields so that deaf people could have direct access to services rather than always depending on interpreters?

"Definitely, yes. You're absolutely right," Cal said. "Now, in the meantime, won't you please sign up with the local registry of interpreters? Interpret part-time while you look for full-time employment."

Of course I said yes; he winked, and now he could see for himself what this had led to.

"Cal, meet my friend Ildefonso."

Ildefonso crossed his arms and blended in with the wall. I met his eyes and signed, "My friend C." Cal shook his hand with enthusiastic warmth and greeted him with, "Good morning, how are you?" I quickly explained to Cal that Ildefonso didn't understand fluent signing and was just beginning to learn his first language. Cal immediately turned to Ildefonso, ignored me, and continued signing as if I had simply made a casual remark about how we met. He mimed and gestured and used no standard signs. At first Ildefonso stared and responded with his habitual stiffness and open-eyed defensiveness. Within sixty seconds, however, he began to respond with his own gestures and mimed expressions. Cal, via gestures and a rapid progression of facial expressions, asked Ildefonso about his life, his school, and his plans. The gist of his questions was similar to some of mine. Had he

85

ever been in a classroom? How did he get to this country? How did he support himself? What amazed me—no, shocked me—was the speed and fluency of the gesturing. Except for the wealth and variety of his eyebrow and mouth movements, Cal didn't mime or invent a single gesture that I couldn't have thought of, but his expressions flew through his hands ten times faster than mine. He never had to pause to think.

Within five minutes, Cal had asked, and Ildefonso had answered, more questions than Ildefonso and I had in an entire morning. These two deaf beings saw the world, visualized abstractions, and thought with their eyes with a speed and clarity my hearing brain could not approach. My gestures and facial expressions were translations from my native sound-dependent thinking to recently learned foreign skills. I had to learn how to carry subtle meaning on my face instead of in my vocal inflection. Cal didn't share language with Ildefonso any more than I did, but they shared the same visual thinking—deaf vision.

Cal needed to discuss something with Elena and excused himself. I hugged him good-bye and turned to Ildefonso, feeling distinctly inferior. My hearing handicapped me.

I first realized how much more visually adept a deaf person is the first time I nervously rode in a car with a deaf driver. I had accepted the ride home after suppressing my surprise that deaf people were allowed to drive. I had never really thought before about whether hearing was necessary for driving or not. My friend, who was simultaneously signing, watching me sign, and watching the crowded road, pulled to the right and stopped.

"What's wrong?" I signed. Then I heard the siren. Even with our visual conversation demanding his attention, he had seen and reacted to the ambulance's red light before I or the hearing drivers heard its siren.

Not only do deaf minds develop visual skills and visual thinking beyond the usual capacity of a hearing mind, visual thinkers collectively create an amazingly rich visual culture, which is reflected most of all in their signed languages. Like most hearing people, I had never entertained the thought of a unique culture created by deaf people. I first realized that deafness was far more than the inability to hear when I met Aaron Matthews in my beginning ASL course. Aaron, a middle-aged man, slightly stooped and very withdrawn, was the only deaf person in the class. He had lost his hearing in his late thirties, and subsequently his job, his wife, his children, and his friends. He decided to learn ASL and begin a new life. Although he attended class daily and participated in all the exercises, he always seemed to be hiding. He sat in the back row in a corner, his eyes concealed by thick dark glasses.

When Aaron became deaf, he still lived in a hearing world, had a hearing wife, hearing children, and hearing friends, but immediately he was alone. He could no longer hear or understand his family, telephone conversations, friends, or anyone else. He could communicate with neither deaf people nor the hearing society that had been his. He could have fought to stay in the hearing world, through paper, pen, and lipreading, but he chose to learn a new culture and language in which he could fully participate. When I first saw him, he looked old and lonely.

I had just met my first deaf friends in Lou Fant's Visual Poetry class. Sometimes I brought them home with me, and my parents would try to socialize without signs and with only a beginning signer as their interpreter. After a deaf friend left one night, my father began talking about his reactions to the evening. He had never before thought of deafness as such an isolating condition, especially for people born deaf. He had always feared blindness more than deafness, but that evening he changed his mind. "If you suddenly went blind," he said to me, "you could tell me, and I could immediately comfort you and begin to act, both of us engaged verbally in solutions and plans. The blindness would not interfere with our usual communication and our relationship. But just imagine suddenly becoming deaf. You would run out here to tell me, and I would offer consolation and advice, but you would receive nothing of it, or very little. Our communication is what makes us human. I was helpless trying to communicate with Tom tonight. I could say nothing to him and understand nothing from him. It was eerie."

My father's view of a human being in isolation without access to language reminded me of what Dr. A. R. Luria, a Soviet neurologist, wrote after witnessing the struggles of a brain-damaged patient. He concluded in *The Man With a Shattered World,* "Apart from being a means of communicating, language is fundamental to . . . thinking and behavior. . . . He [the patient] had lost what is distinctly human—the ability to use language."

What I began to understand through my father's observations and my encounter with Aaron, I later experienced, vicariously, through the stories of many deaf people I met and through the personal accounts of deaf children and deaf adults in *Deaf in America,* by Carol Padden and Tom Humphries. These present a clear picture of the distinction between audiological deafness and cultural deafness. Audiological deafness is a physical state, the lack of hearing, whereas cultural deafness refers to the linguistic community of signers. They have their own history, traditions, and language, and do not view themselves as "handicapped." A standard practice is to make this distinction by writing deafness with a small letter *d* when referring to physical deafness and using a capital letter for cultural Deafness. The way in which Aaron's self-image changed as he learned ASL was much easier for me to understand after reading Padden and Humphries' examination of many individuals, deaf and hearing, who struggled for self-definition and identity amidst conflicting and confusing ideas of deafness and Deafness. In their book, a Deaf child of Deaf parents wonders what horrible handicap a neighbor is suffering from. He learns the word *hearing* and later, to his surprise, discovers that he's the one who is considered handicapped. Another story tells of a hearing child in a Deaf family who never knew he was hearing but assumed he was just like his parents.

Recently in San Francisco, I met a vivacious, good-tempered deaf woman who continued my instruction. She heard until she was nineteen but had for decades signed and been active with the Deaf community. She corrected me, however, when I referred to her as Deaf, informing me that her Deaf friends made fun of her hearing accent and hearing perspective. They moved the sign "hearing," which rolls forward from the mouth, and signed it instead on the forehead, humorously pointing out that her hearing brain was much more evident than the fact that she did not hear sounds. When she underwent surgery to receive a cochlear implant, an ear operation to restore hearing, her Deaf friends were mystified. "What-for? What-for?" they signed. For someone who identifies with the Deaf culture, it is foreign and ludicrous to desire hearing.

When I first met Deaf people, I would have never understood this. My ignorance of Deaf culture prevented me from understanding almost every signed joke I saw. Translation from ASL to English didn't help, because I still thought of Deaf people as people who couldn't hear, and the punch lines always related to cultural differences. Finally I began to catch on when someone joked about a mixed marriage between a hearing woman and a Deaf man. At the same time, no one took any notice of a black and white couple, because they were both Deaf.

Language, I realized, is a membership card for belonging to a certain tribe. The tribe is defined by the language, so the two are inseparable. Within the tribe, members notice and exaggerate differences between families and neighborhoods, such as physical features, dialect variations, and changes in vocabulary. They forget how much more similar than different they are until they meet someone outside the tribe who can't tell any of them apart. Recently I was touring Basel, in German-speaking Switzerland, when a little old man inched his way toward me with quick mincing steps. I didn't notice him until I turned and found we were almost nose to nose. In English, with a tinge of European accent, he asked me where the cathedral was. After I gave him what little information I had, he thanked me and asked if I were English. "No,

I'm American," I exclaimed, in surprise. "Oh, same thing," he responded, waving his hand as if to scold me for wasting his time with trivial distinctions.

On the same trip I stayed at a hotel in Paris an English friend had recommended to me. During my stay, I heard every conceivable English dialect. People from all over the United Kingdom, North America, Australia, and New Zealand were checking in or out or requesting something at the desk. Almost no other nationalities were represented. Word-of-mouth traveled via a specific tribal language and had nothing to do with geography. These two experiences confirmed what Aaron and others since have taught me about language and one's place in a tribe.

With deaf people, an additional complication arises when cultural or tribal differences occur in the same family. Teachers, counselors, doctors, and parents tend to assume that deaf children are native speakers of their family's and country's language. This common supposition is made unconsciously by almost all of us who cannot conceive of deafness from birth. Can anyone truly imagine deafness? We can close our eyes and sympathize with the blind, but we cannot close our ears. We cannot unlearn our language. Aaron's life is certainly different from that of a deaf baby's, but his deafness nonetheless created a barrier within a family, great enough that he chose to transfer to another tribe.

On the other hand, Ildefonso—the man without a tribe—had been given no choice. He shared language and culture with no one.

8

CHAPTER

■■■

MY WORRIES ABOUT HOW TO CONTINUE finding ideas, materials, and lesson plans for Ildefonso proved to be unnecessary. He himself demanded his long-awaited feast. He was starved for all the information that language could feed him. His brain, full of twenty-seven years of experience and stimulation, had kept busy, building as much sense of the world as an isolated mind could. He had the tools of a scientist: observation and deduction. Like a scientist, he had collected information through his senses and figured out a good deal, but, like the first scientist, he had no previous records and no information or resources outside of his sensory input. Now he saw access to what he couldn't discover on his own. I let him lead, initiate, and ask. He was more than ready to learn.

Just as he reviewed the room the minute he understood the meaning behind the symbol *cat*, he must also have reviewed everything that had passed before him. He was ready to restructure his life with meaning and explanations from his new-found magic, language. As he learned language, he could play back his memories like video tapes and replace all those senseless mouth movements, scribbles, typed notes, and signs with meaning. He was full of questions and wanted explanations for thousands of confusing incidents. So I let him outline the course.

We worked on the vocabulary needed to answer the questions that he mimed and I guessed. Some signs he grasped and added to his repertoire easily, while others took several or many lessons to explain. Week, month, and year still seemed impossible for him to learn. In addition to the most basic vocabulary, we needed something more than lists. I kept encouraging phrases, combining signs. So, for example, I used "grass," a new sign, with an adjective right after its introduction.

"Grass green," I repeated.

"Green?" Ildefonso immediately began the green story, but this time he had a few signs to help me interpret the parts he mimed. "Men run frightened me, try to hide, arms grabbed, men look in pockets, friend pockets look in paper." He mimed driving, wandering or looking, and something about running. He lost me again. This time I understood a few pieces, but we went on misunderstanding each other. Ildefonso started again, first miming work. It looked like picking up something and putting it in a container. Then he repeated the running and hiding and "men green" and the pockets and search and "paper." He described a small rectangle with his index fingers, the size of a driver's license. He followed this with "green" and repeated his mime for terror and hiding. Imaginary men searched his pockets and looked for paper. Green men, green truck—and the Green Card! Of course! The Border Patrol with their green uniforms, green cars, and green trailers and buses.

He was an illegal resident. He must have been picked up half a dozen times by Border Patrol men when he was a farmworker. At that time, Ildefonso knew nothing of political boundaries or immigration or law. He still knew nothing except what he had pieced together by himself. He had seen people avoid capture by showing a piece of paper overlaid with green lines to men dressed in green who drove green cars. The sign and symbol "green" could not mean a general color to Ildefonso; green men were too important in his life, having the power to transport him to a place where there was less work and less food. Without knowing how or why, Ildefonso knew that the lack of a Green Card could mean starvation.

Some time later, I impulsively stopped on the highway at a Border Patrol check point. I was totally ignorant of the process by which persons were arrested, determined to be illegal residents, and deported. I was curious. I wanted to know what interactions Ildefonso had had with these green men. If it had been the usual questioning and detention process, I would have an idea of some of Ildefonso's previous experiences with people trying to communicate with him. Perhaps I could get another clue to what the world looked like to him. I walked into the trailer by the highway and saw a blue-eyed blond boy in a green uniform sitting back in his chair with his long legs up on the desk. He looked about sixteen. He tensed and straightened a little in his chair but kept his feet on the desk. Nervously, he asked if he could help me.

I explained that I had met a man without language who told me about his encounters with green men. I was writing about this man, and it would help me to understand more about his life if I knew how the Border Patrol worked.

"How do you know this man had anything to do with immigration officials?" the boy asked. I repeated the "green" story that Ildefonso had told me while wondering what impression Ildefonso would have had of this tall Aryan.

"How do you know this man's an illegal resident?" he persisted. "I mean, we have to go to school to learn how to know if someone's an illegal resident."

"Well, I just assumed he was, because his story implied that he had been arrested, but I don't really know what happened. That's why I stopped. Maybe you could tell me what your job is, how you proceed to find and arrest and deport illegal farmworkers. Then I would be able to interpret his story better." Because he looked at me suspiciously, I explained that I wasn't really interested in the Border Patrol itself, just in this man's life.

"You say you're writing a book about this man, but how do I know you're not a reporter? I'm not supposed to be talking to anyone. You need to talk to my superior. I'll give you directions to the local headquarters."

After his superior tested me with lie-detector questions for almost an hour, he finally gave me a description of the typical procedure for apprehending, detaining, and determining the citizenship of a suspected illegal resident. If Ildefonso had gone through a similar process, someone in green must have questioned him individually several times, then tried again with an interpreter. By law, no one can be deported with evidence based on information gained from another person. Ildefonso had to answer the questions himself.

"Since that was impossible, what would be the next step?" I asked.

"First of all, we make sure the deafness or lack of

understanding is legitimate. We've had people fake deafness before. One time I took a deaf man to the Riverside School for the Deaf to see if anyone there could interpret. They told me he had no language and didn't understand any of my questions. We worked with the Mexican authorities until a relative claimed him. Actually, we run across languageless persons all the time, and we have to advertise on both sides of the border until a friend or relative comes forward."

"How many languageless people do you find?" I asked in astonishment.

"Babies. Frequently we find babies, separated from the parents," he explained casually, and went on to say that until a relative could be found to answer questions pertaining to citizenship, the baby or disabled person was detained, sometimes for weeks. Ildefonso must have had a most perplexing life.

Ildefonso had never indicated to me that he thought his arrests and deportations were possibly unjust, or that his starving family's situation was unfair. He seemed to assume that some system or plan, some reason, existed, and that he was incapable of figuring it out, along with so much of his life. He believed life was confusing only because he didn't understand the rules. He wanted to learn about everything, so he could figure out how to live better. If he could learn enough about avoiding green men, he could work and earn money and support himself.

This one sign and its associations were so important to him, so much a part of his life, that he could not understand how I failed to grasp his "green" story and "green" problem. Instead, I insisted on treating it as if it were just another color. It perplexed him. Sometimes these new symbols worked so well. He could sign "school," and the symbol magically conjured up the entire classroom, campus, students, teachers, and all that he was learning. Why didn't "green" transfer as much information to my head? Suddenly, I remembered my nephew learning to speak. He tried to communicate an entire event with one word. Sometimes it worked. A personal name or pointing to a car could describe the activities of the previous day. Even an adult with language can be swamped with associations and stories attached to one name, such as the name of one's birthplace. All of us have single words powerful enough to carry us to other times and places.

Ildefonso had hoped that all words could be that powerful, containing not only the thing named, but everything attached to it. He barely distinguished between a name and a descriptive word. "Green" was both greenness and all the things related to his experience with green. Weren't green men and green experiences inherent in the symbol? He might repeat my signs and demonstrate some understanding of the meaning, but what was in his head? He might interpret my "Book green" as book and greenness *and* the significance of green experiences. Perhaps the book was about "green" events. All my speculation couldn't help me understand Ildefonso's thinking.

I taught him the name for colors, "color," and for the next few days pointed out the color of everything. I asked him routinely what color various things were, and he answered with his first two-sign sentences. After three or four days, he understood what "color" meant. He signed "color" for the first time, then put his wrist and hand next to mine. He pointed from one to the other and gestured, "What's-this-about?" signing "color" again.

I sat staring helplessly at his expectant face. He had no idea how big the answer was to his question. How could I explain ethnicity and racism in mime and the vocabulary of a two-year-old? He repeated the question by pointing to a black student and signing "color" again.

How could I begin? If I started with geography, he would have to learn what a map is. His three-dimensional world had never been represented in two dimensions. Taking out a piece of paper, I sighed and started. I drew the table, Ildefonso, Susan, and the room. "Room," I explained, signing it very big and then smaller and smaller, until it was the size of the room on the paper. I took another piece of paper and drew the school. "School, cafeteria, room, grass," I pointed out on my map. On another piece of paper, I made the school smaller and added the bus stop and the closest streets and intersections. The next map showed other landmarks, downtown, and some hills. The next map showed farms beyond the hills on one side and the ocean on the other. I brought in pictures to help indicate different places. For two days I drew map after map, representing larger and larger areas until I could include Mexico.

Assuming that Ildefonso had been deported at least once from California, I described Tijuana, the crowded city where the green men took him. Ildefonso began to learn of boundaries drawn by humans instead of nature. The ocean and mountains were not the only barriers separating peoples. He learned about white-skin land and brown-skin land, the political entities called countries, which were named the United States of America and the United States of Mexico.

Finally he knew enough details and could recognize a representation of a large enough area for us to study a real map of North America. With the aid of pictures of California and Mexico, Ildefonso learned geography. I asked him to describe what he did on farms. For the first time, he understood a question instantly. He guessed that I was going to try to figure out his travels. From the mimed descriptions of farmwork, I guessed the crops and where he might have traveled: apple-picking—Washington; potatoes—Idaho; grapes, tomatoes, and cotton—California. I matched pictures of the various plants with their homes. Ildefonso was fascinated and memorized everything as fast as I could give him the information.

We made and studied maps for a week until he was ready for more than a continent. I showed him giant maps hung on a roll from the ceiling. Starting with the now-familiar western American coast, we reviewed his new names: ocean, mountain, river, city, nation, United States, California, Mexico, Los Angeles. Ildefonso stared, mesmerized. He repeated everything with a question on his face, "California? Mexico City?"

"Yes," I responded. Finally I could begin to answer the question he had asked over a week ago. I put the back of my hand next to the back of his hand. "Native American (in ASL, this sign is not related to the ambiguous name *Indian* but refers only to the natives of America)," I signed, and pointed to him. "White," I signed, and pointed to me. "A long, long time ago," I emphasized by repeating, enlarging, and slowing the only tense sign he understood, "whites here (I pointed to Europe); a long time ago, Native Americans here," and I passed my flat hand over all of the Americas. I pointed to a black man in the room, then pointed to Africa. "A long time ago, blacks here." I pointed to an Asian student and then to China. Ildefonso went back to Europe, then North America, looked confused, and signed, "White?" What a question.

With my right hand spread crablike over Europe, I signed "white" with my left hand. I lifted my right hand, keeping my hand rigid as if I had picked up a great crowd, and crossed the Atlantic Ocean. The crowd landed on New England. The left hand swept over the Americas, and the right hand signed "natives." I mimed fighting between the whites and the natives, and with my flat hand I formed a wall that slowly took over North America, pushing the natives south. "Now United States—whites, Mexico—natives," I inaccurately summarized. I couldn't give a very thorough account, and Ildefonso missed many details even in my simplification, but it was a start to answering his question.

Ildefonso's eyes grew huge. He wanted me to repeat the story several times. I repeated that it was a long time ago when the natives filled the continent and there were no white people. He swept his hand over the Americas: "Natives?" he asked, and pointed to his wrist.

"Yes," I answered, "a long time ago." He turned back to the map. His facial muscles were tense as he studied the strange new shapes. He said nothing more. He stood and stared and stared.

Ildefonso told me months later that his leisure activity was watching people. He found crowded places, sat in a central location by a fountain or sculpture, and watched the pedestrians, studying the way they dressed, walked, talked, and touched. He saw giggling, kissing, playing,

and fighting, human games in which he could not participate. His first history lesson and our other dialogues
began to eliminate some of the mystery of the human
interactions he liked to observe. I wished his first lessons
had been on the ideals of Athenian democracy or the
peace-loving Hopi tribe or the greatest inventions and
discoveries in history, instead of green men and the unfor-
tunate significance of the color of one's skin.

9

CHAPTER

■■■

ILDEFONSO'S ONE-SIGN QUESTIONS gave me a hint of
the capacity of an individual human mind that had always
thought in isolation. I knew that I would never be able
to imagine that kind of isolation, and I daily wished that
he could learn language faster so that I could learn more
about his unique conclusions and impressions.

I continued to try to fathom what his thinking had
been like without language, to imagine his aloneness. The
closer I could get to understanding his world, the easier
it would be to explain mine to him. Where, I wondered,
could I find clues to help me. There must be someone
else who had experienced such solitude. As I tried to
think of one, I remembered the story of Ishi, the last
wild Indian in North America. After all the rest of his
tribe, the Yahi, were killed, Ishi, the last speaker of his
language, lived alone for two or three years. In August
1911, out of desperation, starvation, and loneliness, he
wandered from his tribal territory into the corral of a
slaughterhouse near Oroville, California. Like Ildefonso,
he chose to explore unknown territory rather than remain
alone.

Theodora Kroeber, the wife of the anthropologist

who became a friend and caretaker of Ishi, wrote Ishi's biography. She describes the nature of human beings as "social, intermingling, and generalized," and comments that babies "without hearing human speech or experiencing normal emotional expression and exchange" would either die early or not develop distinctively human attributes such as speech. She adds, "Nor do adults thrive in solitude." There is no question that both Ishi and Ildefonso could not thrive in their respective isolation, but hadn't Ildefonso developed human attributes without language and normal expression?

In *The Man With a Shattered World,* Luria writes that "what is distinctly human [is] the ability to use language." One can easily alter this truth so that instead of thinking of language as a distinct human attribute, one thinks of language as a definition of humanness. I cannot conceive of human life without language, and therefore I cannot imagine humanness without language. Yet, from the first day I met Ildefonso, I never doubted his human nature. Although his attempts to communicate reminded me of a mimicking chimpanzee, and he could express little more than a cat or dog, I knew he had human intelligence, a human personality, and an awareness of himself as human. I can understand Ishi more than I can understand Ildefonso, but *my* lack of understanding does not subtract from Ildefonso's humanness.

Some people might find Ishi primitive or barbaric, but only the most bigoted would consider him nonhuman. On the other hand, many people have regarded languageless persons as outside the human race. The ancient Greeks called non-Greeks *bar-bars,* the derivation of the word *barbarians,* because foreign words sounded to them like nonsense syllables. But they recognized that *bar-bars* were not only human but capable of becoming civilized and cultured by learning Greek. They had a phrase *hellenísthenai ten glossan,* which means literally to become hellenized through the Greek tongue. The ancients perceived what Ildefonso taught me. Language does not determine the species; it determines the tribe.

As I mentally compared Ishi and Ildefonso, I found that their similarities revealed their human nature, and their differences showed the importance of language and of belonging to a tribe. Both lived alone and outside of society and could be described as wild men. Both felt the human need to belong, to attach themselves to other human beings, and both met a new and mysterious world because they searched for human contact. In Ishi's mind, this was even at the risk of being killed: "[He] expected in those first days to be put to death. He knew of white men only that they were the murderers of his own people. It was natural that he should expect, once in their power, to be shot or hanged or killed by poisoning," Kroeber explains. Ishi did not eat, drink, or sleep during his first days in the hands of white men.

Ishi and Ildefonso were not simply foreigners traveling to new cultures. They were aliens experiencing the impossibility of time travel. In science fiction, many characters have jumped backward or forward to a different century or millennium. Now in this century, by very different means, two real men suddenly arrived in the modern world as aliens from another age. Ishi came from an ancient culture, from the forgotten era of hunter-gatherers; Ildefonso, from a world resembling that of a prelingual caveman. Kroeber writes of Ishi's journey, "Ishi completed a trip out of the Stone Age into the clang and glare of the Iron Age—a place of clocks and hours and a calendar; of money and labor and pay; of government and authority; of newspapers and business." Her description could also apply to Ildefonso, for although he had witnessed modern life, he had not been able to understand what he saw.

In contrast to Ildefonso, who had no clues as to how to interpret what he saw, Ishi understood the concepts of culture, social structures, and systems of relating. No matter how strange modern culture appeared, he knew that sense and order must exist in it and could be explained. Even though Ishi's language and culture dealt with an aboriginal world, he had lived as part of a community. Although he had had no contact with another human being for years, he had the tools and the help of the minds of his people. He carried the memories of all the people in his life. Their words, information, and advice fed his thoughts and perceptions. Language provides a kind of immortality. Ishi's people, even after death, continued to help him survive and interpret life. Unlike Ildefonso, he had a system of beliefs, ideas, and assumptions that could be used to process the new information from the strange world around him. He could make analogies and comparisons, manipulating all the symbols and ideas that his language had given him.

He possessed what Luria refers to as an inner life. "Regardless of how primitive or abbreviated language may be," Luria writes, "it is pivotal to cognition; by means of it we designate numbers, perform mathematics, calculations, analyze our perceptions, distinguish the essential from the inessential, and form categories of distinct impressions. Apart from being a means of communicating, language is fundamental to perception and memory, thinking and behavior. It organizes our inner life." Ildefonso had had some sort of inner life, but without language and information, thoughts and ideas from others, it could not be complete. Even the lonely last speaker of a language was connected to others in a way that languageless Ildefonso could not be. Ildefonso could relate individually to nature, friends, and family, but he failed to understand most group and functional relationships, especially those that come with modern technology, politics, and easy mobility.

In some ways, a languageless person stays aboriginal. Ildefonso didn't have the tools, the symbols, for abstraction, and had no choice but to touch or move concrete objects. He was limited in his abilities to count in the abstract and could be only functional. Ishi and other aboriginal persons, although capable of counting in the abstract, do not choose to. I wondered if Ildefonso would stay like Ishi after learning language, or if his interest in abstract games and exercises would expand. He would certainly be more susceptible to the pressure to conform than Ishi because he was alone. Ishi had beliefs and habits shared by many for hundreds of years. He had pride in his differences and a continuing loyalty to his people and their ways.

Even Ildefonso's lack of a name was closer to Ishi and naming customs of ancient cultures, including the native tribes of California, than to modern life. As Kroeber explains:

Pre-commune China continued into the twentieth century under a system older and more widespread than our own, that of clan identification by which a baby is born into the clan of the father. This clan becomes his own lifetime clan, with strict taboo against marrying within his clan however numerous and scattered its membership. Sooner or later, someone in the family gives the new baby a personal, private name or nickname, perhaps more than one. This, too, was the Yana practice.

The stranger . . . outside the slaughter house was nameless.

The wild man . . . said that he had been alone so long that he had had no one to give him a name—a polite fiction, of course. A California Indian almost never speaks his own name, using it but rarely with those who already know it, and he would never tell it in reply to a direct question.

He became known as Ishi, which simply means *man* in Yana. He never revealed his private name.

My satisfaction upon hearing Ildefonso's name, and my assumption that everyone has or needs a personal name, was based on a very recent Western custom. The practice, now restricted to Congress, to refer to fellow congressmen as "the gentleman from New Hampshire" or "my friend from Georgia" instead of by name, used to be common.

Of course, Ishi's namelessness and Ildefonso's namelessness were different, but Ishi's way of thinking made me realize that Ildefonso's ability to describe a person, instead of naming him, might seem quite natural to some cultures. Indeed, intertribal communication may have been close to the mime and gestures of Ildefonso.

Not just personal names but names in general may be a later invention than other parts of speech, if language developed in such stages. I can picture our ancestors miming a giant beast with hair and tusks before discovering the time-saving utterance or sign for mammoth.

Names and language organize more than our inner lives. Language influences and, to some extent, determines our perceptions and understanding of the world. Ishi's confusion about the modern world didn't stem simply from ignorance, but from a different picture of the world and the way things are supposed to be. But at least he had a complete picture. Ildefonso could not have organized a coherent view of the world or have imagined one. E. F. Schumacher, in *Small Is Beautiful,* writes:

> First of all, there is language. Each word is an idea. If the language which seeps into us during our Dark Ages [childhood] is English, our mind is thereby furnished by a set of ideas which is significantly different from the set represented by Chinese, Russian, German, or even American.

We may not know anything about the views and ideas of Chinese or Yahi people, but we know a set of ideas exists. When Ildefonso and I first met, Ildefonso had no concept of shared ideas. He could not express his thoughts, and he also could not listen—that is, anticipate any meaning in others' expressions. In contrast, Ishi, who couldn't understand any language spoken to him, knew what conversations and questioning were. "Ishi listened patiently but uncomprehendingly," Kroeber says, describing Ishi's first encounters in Oroville. Later, an anthropologist read a list of Northern and Central Yana words, hoping that if Ishi were from the Southern Yana tribe, he would

understand something. Ishi listened carefully and attentively even though the first word he understood came
quite far down the list. He knew that an exchange of ideas
was possible, and he waited for the key to be found.
Ildefonso had never experienced this kind of exchange.
He performed and copied and guessed at my expecta-
tions, but he had no clue that listening could be valuable.

His mirroring was the single most frustrating obstacle to communication, leading me to blurt out, "No,
watch." Instantly, I regretted it. I was impatient to begin
the dialogue and failed to realize how truly impossible it
must have seemed to Ildefonso.

He continued to stand by himself, within himself,
even after he had the beginnings of language. Still separated and alone, he watched others interact, but he
would not. He expressed the desire to belong, but also
his fear of rejection. I wondered about his sense of self
and whether the boundary between self and others is
wider without language. Even after he knew what communication was, he could not understand what was being
communicated. I encouraged him to greet other students
and taught him a few social amenities—"How are you?"
and "Fine"—but he was too shy to use them. Except for
Cal, who had taken the initiative, he did not try to converse with anyone but me.

He would mime a fast fluent signer, then turn his
body to become another character and mime a clumsy
slow signer. He dropped his jaw and looked stupid, placing his tongue limply between his teeth. Then he pointed
to himself. He concluded by signing, "Embarrassed me,"
using a new sign from a recent lesson. I showed my dis-
approval of the stupid face by frowning and shaking my

head. I explained, mostly in mime, the difference between ignorance and stupidity, a lesson that would be repeated for months. Some people, I told him, would gladly communicate with him and understand that he was a beginner and a student. He wasn't ready, and wanted to practice and learn with me first.

He would not participate, but he was fascinated by conversations and studied signers constantly. He began to pick out one or two signs a day and bring them to me for deciphering. Sometimes he guessed a sign's meaning and would surprise me by using it in our mime-sign conversations. One morning, for example, he casually tossed the sign "school" into a mostly mimed description. He had picked it up and guessed its meaning correctly. Other times he would need days or weeks of lessons to provide the background information and additional language before understanding a sign or a phrase. Once he brought in the sign "monthly" and wanted an explanation. The question had to be shelved. He didn't yet understand that we measured time, and he couldn't understand my first lesson on the clock. He could not grasp anything political, social, or scientific; his language was too elementary, and he knew next to nothing of the world.

Often we continued our "lessons"—our dialogues and study of each other's world—through class breaks. Many times we had lunch together, sometimes in the company of other signers, sometimes alone. We began to make it a habit to walk to a neighborhood burrito stand when we wanted to be alone for lunch, to continue an especially sensitive or intense discussion. Outside of the confining classroom, we could be less formal, less like teacher-student and more like friends. Also the practical tasks of ordering lunch were easy vocabulary lessons. I would ask in mime, for example, if he wanted chicken, beef, or beans in his burrito, then replace the mime and gestures with signs as he understood.

Only three weeks after Ildefonso had connected with language, I ordered two chicken burritos at the burrito stand, but when I took out money to pay for them, he pushed my hand down and signed his first, complete ASL sentence of more than three signs: "No, burrito buy I."

"No, (that's) OK, burrito buy I," I argued. I mimed-signed that I worked and earned money and he was in school, so I could buy the burritos.

He mimed mowing a lawn and receiving money, then repeated, "Burrito buy I."

"Put your money in your pocket for later," I mimed and signed, then realized he didn't understand "later." "Burrito buy I," I insisted.

"No!" his fingers snapped; "God, friend. Burrito buy I."

Did I see that correctly? Not only had he signed his most complicated thought to date, without any mime, but "God"? Where did he find that sign, and how did he leap to such an incredible guess on how to use it? He connected God and friend and placed them above burrito buying. His anger was that of a religious instructor. I was properly rebuked for my concern for the material world. Who had more money was trivial. Buying a burrito was only significant as an act of friendship.

Later he asked me what did the sign "God" mean, specifically. He had guessed correctly that it stood for unseen greatness, apart from and more important than the tangible stuff in front of us. I couldn't add anything

to his use of "God," because we didn't have enough language between us to discuss the difference between religion and physics or individual beliefs and common
assumptions.

Without language or input from another, this isolated
mind   invented/imagined/realized/perceived—which   is
the right verb?—two separate realms. With no education
of any kind, he expressed a basic theme found in every
religion and in literature from all times and places.

What is in our heads before language integrates the
collective human mind with our individual thoughts?
How was Ildefonso's contrast different from the ancient
Greeks' distinction between zoa (physical life) and psyche
(spiritual life), the ancient Hebrews' double meaning of
Zion, or Jesus's comparisons of two kingdoms?

Could his attachment of meaning to the sign "God"
really be an independent thought? I began to realize that
anything Ildefonso expressed could be an answer to one
of two questions: What can an individual mind create?
or, How much culture and even abstract thinking can be
communicated without language? What had his mother
or father or priest taught him with pictures and mime?
How much enculturation depends on language, and how
much is independent? We are all taught eye contact and
social distances and many other specific rules of behavior
visually and unconsciously. Naturally, Ildefonso learned
those rules. What else had he learned without symbols?

Ildefonso's mind contained the answers. Everything
in his head not invented by him got there through nonverbal communication or observation. If he hadn't
thought of a higher or nonmaterial entity called God, had
he learned this idea in Mexican Catholic churches? He

must have seen people kneel and pray to images and to the ceilings of cathedrals. In Mexico, he would have seen people cross themselves and look upward, many times, perhaps even regularly in his home. How did his active mind store all the millions of unrelated pieces of information, and what did he believe about things seen and unseen? How could a religious belief be any different from most of his ideas? To him, mysterious forces controlled the whole world. Was church any stranger than interactions at a bank? What sense did he make out of his observations of weddings or funerals or the Day of the Dead, an annual event in southern Mexico when people dress as skeletons and representations of death?

Ildefonso's first sentence made me more curious about his languageless life than all his silence had.

He bought the burrito.

10

CHAPTER

■ ■ ■

ONE MORNING AS I CONTINUED an exercise to practice the preposition signs "on," "in," and "under," Ildefonso interrupted. He made signs and gestures in the air, then wiped them out by quickly shaking his hands back and forth while frowning. He pointed to some paper, placed it in front of him, and picked up a pencil, looking at me expectantly. He wanted to try words again. A new list began to form. *Cat,* of course, headed the column, and I showed him the words for the signs I had just taught him. *On* and *in* were short and easy, but Ildefonso still made mistakes. I thought the problem was handwriting; he needed more practice.

The next day he completely misunderstood a simple word I fingerspelled. When he repeated it, he replaced the *e* with an *o.* After I showed him the mistake, he still mixed up the vowels. I asked for the new list of words he brought home to practice. I studied the errors. He never consistently showed the difference between the letters *a, o,* and *e.* I thought of a reading disorder, but remembered other mistakes with fingerspelling that didn't seem related to his vowel confusion. I noticed, for example, that he confused *I* and *Y, G,* and *H* (the respective pairs have similar handshapes). Being extremely nearsighted myself, I wondered if Ildefonso had a vision problem.

Elena arranged for an eye exam, and my suspicion was confirmed, but the diagnosis proved useless. Ildefonso didn't have more than a few dollars, and his illegal residency status prohibited access to any social services. He obviously was able to learn some signs and words despite his poor vision, but it certainly slowed him down. Glasses, I discovered, would cost twenty-four dollars. Between Ildefonso and me, we might be able to squeeze out six or seven.

Twenty-four dollars was not a great amount, but John and I were in debt. I had been able to postpone looking for a full-time job in order to teach Ildefonso, but now John's student loan had run out. That night I couldn't stop thinking about Ildefonso's glasses. What could we sell? I looked around at our three pieces of second-hand furniture. There was nothing of value. I briefly contemplated going from door to door, explaining the situation and asking for donations, but rapidly decided that no one would believe my story or care about an illegal resident who was languageless, deaf and mute. I had no choice but to continue with yet another obstacle and my lowered morale.

Ildefonso's vision problems must have made his life and understanding even more difficult, which made me admire him even more for all that he had been able to learn and achieve. I became increasingly anxious about the end of our course together, which was approaching rapidly. I could not postpone a full-time job much longer. It grieved me not to be able to afford to buy Ildefonso glasses, but it grieved me more to know that I could not afford many more weeks with him.

11

CHAPTER

■■■

WHILE I WAS ALL TOO AWARE of time passing, Ildefonso showed no concern, as if our talks and mornings together would continue forever. He had no concept of time as we learn it.

The subject first came up during our second week together—Ildefonso's first week of language. His vocabulary, with the exception of *cat,* was the names of things in view: chair, table, book, door, and clock. Without thinking, I signed "clock" (literally, *timepiece*) along with furniture names and parts of the room. During that week when Ildefonso met his first names, I was too overwhelmed to reflect on what was most alien to him. Clocks and watches were so much a part of my everyday life, I considered them as familiar as chairs and doors.

One morning Ildefonso saw Elena point to the clock while scolding a habitually tardy student. He pointed to it, shrugged his shoulders, and brought his hands up, asking me to explain why that piece of furniture attracted so much attention. He didn't know the number ten yet, and he didn't know minutes from hours from years. How could I explain time to him? I sat staring at him as he stared back, waiting for the clock lesson.

In those few frozen seconds, I realized how truly abstract a concept time is. It is a lifetime subject for philosophers, physicists, and poets. Our accepted units of measurement for it are almost entirely arbitrary, and what is based on reason the majority of people, including me, accept with only partial understanding. What could I possibly tell a person who had no language and didn't know the earth circles around the sun?

I decided to start with day and night again, to repeat and elaborate on activities during the day and end with sleep for the night. I remembered my three-year-old nephew trying to figure out what *tomorrow* meant. When we tried to explain, he stared off in space, his brain almost audibly clicking as it tried to assimilate this new thought. The only way he could begin to think of time was to connect the action of waking with the return of sunlight: a new day. All children have trouble learning to measure time; it is not a natural idea. With the same explanation that eventually worked with my nephew, I launched another lesson about time. As so often happened, Ildefonso's immediate question had to wait while a series of lessons provided enough background and vocabulary to explain the significance and reason for the clock.

"Time," I signed, the first part of the sign for clock. Ildefonso waited for meaning. So did I.

"Sun," I signed, describing a yellow ball in the sky. Puzzled, he searched for something round on the ceiling. I took him outdoors and pointed to the sun. "Sun." Then I repeated my earlier description of day and night, adding a few new signs that Ildefonso now knew. Ildefonso, arms folded, still waited patiently for meaning.

I tried again, acting out waking and eating, working and stopping to eat again. As I mimed the sun disappearing, I pretended to eat again and prepare for bed. Fortunately, the signs for "morning," "noon," and "afternoon" or "evening" relate to the idea of the changing position of the sun—one arm is the horizon, and one hand represents the sun and moves to different points over the horizon. Unfortunately, it didn't help. Ildefonso's arms and face remained silent.

I recalled my earlier unsuccessful lecture with two columns, one for actions, one for names. Ildefonso shared none of our language categories, whether parts of speech or divisions of time. His inability to understand my lessons on verbs and nouns and now on time did not derive merely from ignorance but from an entirely different view of reality. It struck me that his view could be just as legitimate as mine. Benjamin Whorf, one of the first modern linguists, thought that language creates illusions and false categories, including my idea of action words. He points out that "English pattern treats 'I hold it' exactly like 'I strike it,' 'I tear it," . . . Yet 'hold' in plain fact is no action, but a state of relative positions." My division between nouns and verbs was not so logical or obvious as I had thought. I had even more doubts about teaching anything sensible about time.

Ildefonso was like the hypothetical man referred to by Whorf in *Language, Thought and Reality*:

Consider how the world appears to any man, however wise and experienced in human life, who has never heard one word of what science has discovered about the Cosmos. To him the earth is flat; the sun and moon are shining objects of small size that pop up daily above an eastern rim, move through the upper air, and sink below a western edge; obviously they spend the night underground. The sky is an inverted bowl made of some blue material. The stars, tiny and rather near objects, seem as if they might be alive, for they "come out" from the sky at evening like rabbits or rattlesnakes from their burrows, and slip back again at dawn. "Solar system" has no meaning to him, and the concept of a "law of gravitation" is quite unintelligible—nay, even nonsensical. For him bodies do not fall because of a law of gravitation, but rather "because there is nothing to hold them up"—i.e., because he cannot imagine their doing anything else. He cannot conceive space without an "up" and "down" or even without an "east" and "west" in it. For him the blood does not circulate; nor does the heart pump blood. . . . Cooling is not a removal of heat but an addition of "cold"; leaves are green not from the chemical substance of chlorophyll in them, but from the "greenness" in them. It will be impossible to reason him out of these beliefs.

Whorf, of course, never imagined that his description could fit a real person. It wasn't that Ildefonso didn't understand the coming and going of light and dark or the habit of waking; he didn't see why he should care about it.

In spite of my doubts and speculations, I continued with time lessons. Ildefonso began to sign, "Good morning" and "noon-meal." He worked on clock exercises and could soon associate a few times with different activities, but when I wanted to move from the parts—morning, noon, and night—to one day as an entity, he completely lost interest. The idea of counting time like counting stones or crayons seemed distasteful to him. He showed much more interest in and curiosity about other subjects. Communication did, however, improve as he gradually accepted the most general signs for the past, the present, and the future, but I gave up trying to teach him to count days.

Only a week after I had stopped the time lessons, I discovered that Ildefonso's birthday was in mid-December. In less than a month, he would be twenty-eight. All of his years were unmarked and undifferentiated, but this one, I hoped, would be numbered and celebrated. Birthdays and holidays never had had and never would have meaning for him without the knowledge of seasons and years. For the first and only time, I ignored his desire to move to other topics and insisted on teaching him about time.

I tried to explain seasonal changes, until I realized that this explanation was lost on someone raised in southern Mexico. He must have noticed periods of rain, times of extreme heat and dryness, and spells of cooler weather, but he wouldn't necessarily have realized that they were sequential or cyclic. The changes had not been drastic or sudden as they are in New England or the Midwest. I mimed farmwork and harvesting different crops, ending with picking apples in the autumn. I added notes about the weather changing and the lengthening and shortening of the day as I picked my various fruits and vegetables. I described empty fields, sowing and watering these fields, and their coming to life with green. Ildefonso followed the descriptions, but failed to see where I was leading him with these familiar scenes. I repeated the farming cycle but made clear distinctions between each set of activities and placed them in a row like boxes, from left to right. Then, as if picking up four blocks from end to end, my hands became two walls describing the sets of farming activities as one unit. "Year one," I signed, then quickly added another series of identical activities and continued with "Years two . . . years three."

Ildefonso looked at me blankly. He reminded me of the clown in Shakespeare's *Twelfth Night* who sings, after describing his life, "With hey, ho, the wind and the rain; For the rain it raineth every day." It happened again and again and wasn't otherwise worth noting. Ildefonso acknowledged the importance of registering the wind and the rain, but he had no concern about *when* they came.

I went back to my mime routine of the children— little Susan and little Ildefonso—which followed his "dumb me" statement. Using the general past sign, I reversed time and shrank Susan and Ildefonso until they were babies. I repeated the past sign and continued backward in time until I came to their two pregnant mothers. Then I moved time forward again with the general future sign. The mothers grew bigger until they gave birth to the two babies. I stopped, pointed to the clock and to a calendar, and signed, "Age zero." Time moved forward again with the future sign, and the babies lengthened; "Age—year one." The babies grew into toddlers: "Age— years two." I added years as the children grew until they reached adult height, and I stopped at age twenty. I pointed to myself and signed, "Age—years twenty-four; Ildefonso, age you—twenty-seven." I started time up again, and Susan and Ildefonso became older, tireder, and eventually bent and wrinkled. "Age—years fifty; years sixty; years seventy; years eighty," I signed as we declined.

Ildefonso looked interested. He didn't understand what "year" or "age" meant, but I think he understood that there was a way by which we measured a person's growth and changes.

I decided practice with measurements might help broaden his understanding. We left time and worked with a ruler and tape measure for a few days. We measured everything in sight, including our heights. Ildefonso enjoyed this since he could combine it with addition and subtraction, which were still his favorite exercises. The ruler also gave him the chance to practice equivalents, such as twelve inches equal one foot. I hoped these might help with the much more difficult time concepts—seven days equal one week, four weeks equal one month, and so on.

When we resumed the time lessons, we concentrated on "tomorrow" and "yesterday." I drilled Ildefonso on activities and conversations that happened the day before. I began to ask him what he had for lunch "yesterday," and had he practiced the new signs from "yesterday." I ended each lesson with "See you tomorrow." It worked. In a few days he had adopted "yesterday" and "tomorrow"—his first references to days as units of time.

The names of the days of the week followed, a lesson that had failed completely only three weeks before. He memorized all the names but continued to make mistakes. Weekends always confused him. I think he must have showed up at the school once or twice on Saturday or Sunday. Slowly, he accepted that the two-day break consistently came between what I called Friday and Monday.

That seven days equal a week seemed a useless fact to Ildefonso, especially since he was still struggling to master the names of the seven days. By using "week-last" and "week-next" in the same way as "yesterday" and "tomorrow," he began gradually to accept the idea of week. I don't think he had the idea of seven days, since he used "week" almost as a synonym for Fridays and Mondays— that is, something that came before and after the weekend.

He showed no interest in "month" and began to lose patience with me. I repeated the history of babies growing to adults and added the question: How can one count from one year to twenty years? With the calendar, I showed him one year, made up of days, weeks, and months. I raised the babies again, counting off days, weeks, and years. His interest grew, but the calendar still didn't seem half as useful or interesting as inches and feet.

Right after his introduction to calendars, the class celebrated someone's birthday. Ildefonso must have seen many celebrations before, but he had never known what they were about. I explained that the day, month, and year were noted at birth, and the day was celebrated every year during the person's life. It was, I taught him, a "birthday." He understood and finally accepted the practice of counting time, at least for the sake of birthday celebrations.

We began to count the days until his birthday. The closer it came, the more excited he appeared. But two days before he looked very worried and asked if anyone else knew. He was afraid there would be no celebration. I assured him that people knew and would not forget.

When the day came, Ildefonso walked into class expecting a great colorful sight. But the classroom looked the same as usual. He didn't say anything, but his eyes swept the room frequently. At lunch time, he looked a little downcast as we walked with the class to the lounge and cafeteria area. I purposely stopped Ildefonso to ask him a question as the class disappeared through a glass door. As Ildefonso started to enter the cafeteria, I stopped him. "We're eating outside today on the patio," I explained, and he followed me out.

He walked into signed shouts of "Happy Birthday," streamers, and his first birthday party. His face broke into a wide smile, and he shyly thanked the crowd. His cake had twenty-eight candles, which he carefully counted before blowing them out. He studiously examined every card, unwrapped his presents, and conscientiously thanked the appropriate person after each card or gift.

As he stood facing his classmates and the cake and decorations, he looked very pleased with himself and his party. As his hands traveled with the sign for "thank-you" to his fellow students, the sun's rays bounced off his birthday present from Elena and the class—his first watch—proudly displayed on his wrist.

12

CHAPTER

∎∎∎

THE STUCCO BUNGALOW WAS AS UGLY and squat as usual, and the Los Angeles sky, blue and cloudless as usual, offered no clues to the season. In Room 6, however, red streamers, giant snowflakes, blue and silver aluminum bulbs, Christmas cards, and a Christmas tree replaced books, paper, and one of the big tables. Elena and three students stood on tables and chairs hanging the decorations. The man with the Afro and two other students struggled to put up the tree next to Elena's office. Mary Ann was smiling and directing people with pointing, waves of her hands, and her nonsense speech. Everyone looked happy and glad of the break from routine except Ildefonso.

He sat in his corner as he had the first week we met, although now he looked more confused than afraid. He had seen Christmas decorations and holiday celebrations before, just as he had seen birthday parties, but to him they were a part of the world's unexplained craziness. He still didn't know what they meant, but now he had access to reason and sense. Answers and explanations waited to be unlocked by his new set of keys: "where," "what,"

125

"who," "how," "why," and his most recent acquisition, "when." His face lit up and his hands rose when he saw me. His questions began before I was even halfway across the threshold.

Three months earlier such a sight would have exhilarated me, but now I was concerned. He relied too heavily on me for answers. He trusted me and my answers more than he did anyone else's, and he could communicate more easily with me. We had learned enough of each other's styles and gestures to be able to complement our elementary signing with our own gestural dialect. I could read Ildefonso's face and mime faster than others could. I knew he would learn much more if he talked to other people, but he was far too shy. His frustrated conversations with other signers increased his doubts about the universality of symbols. He still showed surprise when someone used the same sign I had just taught him. He needed not only to add to the little language he knew by conversing more, but to discover that his questions worked with all ASL signers.

Observing his dependence on me and his discomfort with others, I was reminded of my own discomfort when learning sign language. After a few months in Lou Fant's class, I had gained confidence in my signing and comprehension, and I began to consider myself fluent in casual conversations. Then one day a deaf stranger signed to me, and I understood only a single movement. I was stunned. I couldn't even make a good guess as to what he had said. I realized that Lou Fant, an actor and professor, had extremely clear and articulate signs, even in casual conversation. Also, I had become accustomed to his style and set of facial expressions. I didn't really know

ASL; I knew Lou Fant's beginning signed language. I had to meet the deaf community and learn how different pairs of hands add to and change their language. In the same way, Ildefonso had to expand his field of communicators to learn language. Otherwise, he would be stuck with the simplified, stylized system we had developed out of necessity.

"Tree, colors strung-all-over, mean what?" Ildefonso signed, as he surveyed the room with a frown and outstretched arms, an implicit demand not to leave any details unexplained.

"Christmas," I signed, and repeated it. Ildefonso signed "Christmas," and followed it with "Mean what?"— a perfect ASL sentence for "What does Christmas mean?" I smiled inside every time he signed three signs or more; he had been using language for less than four months. Christmas, I explained, was a birthday celebration like the one he had had the week before, but this time everyone gave presents to everyone else and received presents from everyone. I unthinkingly used his birthday as an easy opening to describe Christmas, but since I still had to act out much of my explanation and use the present tense, I quickly saw problems heading my way.

"Who? Birthday who?" Ildefonso asked. I started to explain the origins of Christmas, but felt uncomfortable looking into his wide-open eyes. He didn't have enough language to understand the difference between religious beliefs and facts about multiplication or political boundaries. Since I couldn't explain the difference between a belief and a fact, he would assume that the idea that Jesus is God's son was as universally accepted as "This is called a chair" and "Blacks came from Africa."

I tried to explain that many people celebrated Christmas because of traditions and customs, but it seemed as useless as trying to explain beliefs in mime. If anything needs language to describe it, it is the collective myths and traditions of hundreds or thousands of years. Ildefonso had just learned the existence of symbols and rarely used more than one or two at a time. Now I had to explain to him an annual set of customs and rituals that included inexplicable symbols: a decorated tree in the living room, cards and presents, Santa Claus and caroling, to name only a few.

Ildefonso wouldn't let me back out. "Who? Birthday who?" he repeated. I told him that a long, long, long time ago, a baby was born in a shed. After he understood the mimed part about where the cows eat and sleep, his face lit up with comprehension, and he motioned for me to follow him. A manger scene had been put on the table next to the Christmas tree. Ildefonso pointed to the manger and gestured, "You mean that one?"

"Yes, long-long-time-ago. Name Jesus," I answered. Before I could continue, Ildefonso was painting a picture in the air of a giant cross, which he then hung himself on. He made the cross in the air again and placed it high above him. He pointed to the cross, then to the manger, and signed "Same?"

I was stunned. How had he made that association? I wondered more and more about the kind of communication he had had with his parents and the people in his village. He undoubtedly had gone to church every Sunday. What did he think of all the icons and pictures, the altar, the incense and priestly robes, the raised silver goblet and white wafers held out to the people filing by?

Was it any stranger to him than watching people reset their clocks or argue on television?

I should learn never to make assumptions. His brain obviously processed more information than I had imagined possible without language. How I wished our days together could continue indefinitely, especially now when we could communicate a little faster. We had so much to teach each other. Every morning my stomach tightened when I remembered how little time we had left. What was the next lesson? How could I list priorities of topics, essential vocabulary, and useful structures? Everything was important.

Ildefonso's uncorrected nearsightedness also frustrated me and slowed his progress. I tried not to think about it. There was nothing I could do except write large letters and fingerspell as slowly and clearly as possible. I noticed that the local rehabilitation counselor for deaf persons visited Elena for several days in a row. I wondered which student was going through a crisis but paid no more attention. A few days later when I walked in, to my surprise and delight, Ildefonso sat with a smug smile on his face and a pair of glasses on his nose. His gold wire-rims gave him a scholarly appearance which I thought quite appropriate.

I soon abandoned my worries about priorities. Ildefonso continued to direct the course as he always had, with his questions. He also began expressing himself more. He wanted to tell me of his life, his plans, and what he was learning outside of our class. He went to a welding class in the afternoon and asked me about welding. He was delighted to find that I knew nothing about welding and immediately showed me different welding techniques and which parts of a ship needed which kind. After making sure that I understood everything, he sat proudly back in his chair.

A few days later he announced that he had been hired for a welding job at a shipyard. He had to leave school, but he assured me he would earn enough money to be able to return. He wanted to keep learning. He needed to learn English words—at least enough to get a driver's license. The end that we both had sensed had come. His reason for leaving made it a little easier. I had dreaded the day I would have to stop. Fortunately for my conscience, Ildefonso quit first.

Our last week together, Ildefonso described himself and his new view of the world. New information and opportunities had given him new goals. He wanted to figure out how to become a legal resident. He could now not only describe a Green Card, he knew what it said and meant. With a Green Card he could get a legitimate and more permanent job. He would earn enough money for food and shelter and then save enough to buy a little place of his own. He still used mime for most of what he told me, but he signed at least a third of his narrative, which helped my understanding tremendously. He paused and frowned and asked me, "Why do people have such big places?" He mimed people grabbing things to their chest and accumulating great possessions, then he described the wealth around us. He compared this to the poverty in Mexico and looked sad and thoughtful. Language didn't help to explain some things in the world.

During winter break, I invited Elena and Ildefonso to supper for a graduation celebration. Ildefonso had successfully completed his first and only semester of education. Introductions and initial greetings passed without problems, except that Ildefonso acted surprised to meet John. He had had no idea I was married. I remembered telling him so once in response to what I thought was a question about my family, but obviously he hadn't understood.

Ildefonso still missed most of the conversation, and he reverted to his former withdrawn posture. He had journeyed the equivalent of light years, but he still had a long distance to go if he was to catch up, especially in social interaction. My sadness at our parting increased as I watched him concentrate on his plate to avoid eye contact and embarrassment.

I hugged both guests good-bye and lost track of Ildefonso for over six months. Then one day, on a street corner, I ran into him at a bus stop. Emotion tightened my throat when I saw him sign. His grammar and vocabulary were still simple, like a young child's, but his arms and hands and face worked together smoothly in new fluid patterns that looked like adult language. He signed with confidence and unhesitating rhythm. His whole stature, including the way he held his metal lunch pail and wore his hard hat, expressed his pride in his new life.

Our short bus conversation renewed our friendship. I invited him to a potluck supper I had scheduled for the next month and gave him directions and the date. He never showed up, and I had no way of contacting him to find out what had happened. A short while later, I moved three thousand miles across the country to North Carolina for John's medical training and my graduate school. I doubted that I would ever hear of Ildefonso again.

13

CHAPTER

■■■

ALTHOUGH I NEVER FORGOT ILDEFONSO, gradually, during the routine tasks of getting through the day, he became a kind of dream, alive during an evening conversation, lost in the next day's traffic jam. More than seven years passed, my marriage ended, and I returned to California, but my curiosity about languageless people remained. Whenever I had the time and the opportunity, I would look through a book about learning language, or ask someone in linguistics, psychology, or adult education if anyone had written about or discussed languageless adults. I found nothing. No one had heard of a languageless adult who was not also severely impaired mentally or psychologically. My questions sat on a back shelf in my mind while I became involved in other things.

Sometimes I read or heard arguments about thinking and language. "Can we think without language?" I heard someone ask. "No, of course not," someone else answered. Everything I read or heard was purely abstract, hypothetical, and speculative. I assumed I was hearing or reading the wrong people and made a mental note to investigate until I found the people who knew more about the subject.

One day I was waiting for a friend at the University of California at Riverside. Having nothing to do, I wandered through the library. Finally I remembered Ildefonso while I was in the right place. I searched through the card catalog, looking up anything I could think of that might apply: language, language learning, language acquisition, languagelessness, alingual, prelingual, deafness. Only five or six entries seemed promising. I checked them, but in spite of titles like *Thinking Without Language,* I found nothing. Authors mentioned only prelingual or languageless children and had no references to adults. There were some astonishing opinions. In Donald Moores's *Psycholinguistics and Deafness* I read:

> The specific ability to develop language appears to peak around the ages of three to four, and tends to steadily decline thereafter. Perhaps any language program initiated after the age of five, no matter what methods are used, is doomed to failure for the majority of deaf children.

In *American Annals of the Deaf,* Edward L. Scouten wrote:

> If syntax is not a functioning aspect of a prelingual deaf child's expressive language after his first five years of schooling, it is likely never to be.

Another researcher declared that the tremendous retardation in language development which handicaps deaf youth cannot be ameliorated. If I had read about language learning and the "doomed to failure" attitude of the experts before meeting Ildefonso, I would probably never have tried to teach him.

I still refused to accept the possibility that Ildefonso was a freak. I decided to continue my search until I found someone else who had learned language as an adult, or someone who had taught a prelingual adult. I made a dozen phone calls, drove hundreds of miles, talked to professors in adult education, linguistics, and psychology, and visited more libraries.

The interviews did not go well. Ildefonso's story was dismissed with questions like, "Was it documented?" and, "Are you a linguist?" One woman, upon hearing my questions, shouted at me, "Who are you?" A graduate student told me, "Nobody's interested in that subject any more— that was popular last century," and advised me to pick another subject if I was thinking about entering a graduate program in linguistics.

Finally I heard of two linguists who were documenting the progress of a prelingual deaf adult learning her first language. I could not get an appointment with either researcher, but I met a graduate student working with one of them. He excitedly told me of the incredible "once in a lifetime" discovery of a prelingual adult. I knew meeting a prelingual adult was not a once-in-a-lifetime occurrence. If it had been, I wouldn't have met three in one classroom. I was definitely looking in the wrong places.

I took my questions out of the universities and onto the streets. Signing Deaf communities share almost any and all information more readily and frequently than the average hearing community, like all cultures that use personal communication for information instead of television, radio, and the printed word. The amount of sharing and repetition had become obvious to me years earlier when I introduced myself to a group of six or seven Deaf people I met at a picnic. Even though everyone saw my name and where I was from in my introduction, the spelling of my English name, my namesign, and California's namesign passed from person to person until everyone was completely satisfied that they had all seen the exact same information.

If one Deaf person had a story of a languageless adult, then almost the entire Deaf community would have added it to their collective repertoire. One can find out almost anything about Deaf people through this word-of-hand network. In addition, many Deaf people have experienced language deprivation in their childhood; to them, it's not such a novel subject.

I remembered one of my first deaf friends, Greg Castillo, who told me his school teachers had punished him for not speaking and lipreading. He had scored very high on a nonverbal IQ test and was supposed to perform as a star pupil, but he never understood what was going on in the classroom or why the teachers angrily shook him and made extreme mouth movements in his face. He began learning his first language at age twelve, after his parents transferred him from the oral school (where sign language or manual communication was forbidden) to a residential school for the deaf. He was on the playground and saw some kids signing, his first exposure to ASL. He didn't understand what they were saying, but he understood that these movements contained meaning and could

135

be deciphered, unlike the tiny lip shapes his parents and teachers used. He took the first step toward language, and, incredibly, he caught up with his peers. He now holds a master's degree in mathematics from California State University at Northridge.

I started my detective work at the university where I had learned sign language and had met Greg. After asking several people with no results, I ran into a Deaf man I knew who worked at the Center on Deafness. He asked me if I remembered the Deaf lawyer in Chicago who defended a languageless deaf man in a murder trial. I had read the story but forgotten it. I could not even remember the name of the lawyer, who later wrote a book about the case. My friend looked through his card file for the name, but halfway through he stopped: "Oh, yes, here's someone . . . Virginia McKinney. I forgot about her. She worked with a man who just showed up at her school one day. He couldn't identify himself or communicate, so he couldn't receive any support or services. Virginia adopted him and taught him language. She named him Joe. The story was written up in the *Los Angeles Times,* but I forget how long ago. Virginia teaches deaf adults downtown. She's the person to talk to."

I called Virginia McKinney and asked about the languageless man she had taught. She said she was too busy to talk to me just then, but if I visited the Center for Communicative Development, which she directed, she would be able to meet with me. I made an appointment, and when I arrived, I walked into a group of signers crowded in the hallway. The main room housed computers and a few tables, a Christmas tree, and about twenty deaf people. No one was attending classes, because this was the last day before the winter break and everyone was preparing for the Christmas party. I talked to a few people, students and teachers, and informed Dr. McKinney's assistant that I was waiting for her. While I was signing with one of the students, I noticed a few individuals sitting on the sidelines watching. I wondered if they were just learning language for the first time. Before I could approach any of them, the assistant motioned to me.

I followed him into an office full of files, books, boxes, computers, teletype machines, cords, miscellaneous hardware, display charts, overflowing bookshelves, and Dr. McKinney seated behind a large desk covered with papers, notebooks, a large full ashtray, and an open box of chocolates. With her left hand she motioned for me to sit in the only empty chair while she puffed away on a cigarette held in her right, ordered her assistant to check on something, asked him a question, crushed her cigarette out on the glass ashtray, lit another, waved the smoke away from her face, and turned to me. "How can I help you? As you can see," she quickly added while surveying her desk, "I'm busy, but I can answer a few questions."

She signed and talked simultaneously, but her signs were sometimes half-formed and sometimes forgotten. Her voice sounded completely normal. I thought she simply signed out of habit. I voiced my introduction without signing. "What?" she asked, and signed, "Sign! I'm deaf."

"Sorry, I didn't know," I apologized. "I heard about Joe and am excited to meet someone who has taught a languageless adult." I briefly explained my experience with Ildefonso, and said, "You are the only person I know of who has taught language to a languageless adult. How did Joe communicate when you first met him?"

I continued signing questions as long as she answered them. I learned about and met Joe, who walked in during our discussion. I was tremendously excited to see someone like Ildefonso, and I wanted to talk to him and ask him all the questions I was waiting to ask Ildefonso. But after a short introduction, Dr. McKinney asked him to leave. At least I had had the opportunity to see him sign and the pleasure of observing in him the same curiosity and interest that Ildefonso had shown. Before he left, he asked who I was, what was going on, and where I came from.

Dr. McKinney answered a few more questions and told me to read her dissertation, which included Joe's introduction to language. Without breaking eye contact, I scribbled notes as fast I could between signing questions. When I commented on how valuable her information was, she sighed, waved her cigarette, and exclaimed that most people remained skeptical. It was not, she explained, that older deaf children or deaf adults couldn't learn or improve their language skills, it was the education system, and she showed me some statistics on the reading skills of deaf high school graduates.

"Have you published anything describing your program here?" I asked.

She looked weary. "Nobody listens. I'm too busy here, as you can see," she sighed and waved her cigarette across the piles of papers on her desk.

"How many students like Joe have you taught here?"

Instead of answering with a number, she began to

tell stories of many languageless deaf students who had learned language at her center. A woman of twenty-one from India who was both deaf and legally blind had no language when she first arrived. Five years later, she was so happy to be able to interpret what she barely saw in the sky, she wrote a spontaneous essay that Dr. McKinney had printed on a poster board:

> Yesterday I saw the rainbow. It had eight colors. It was over the sky yesterday afternoon. I smiled at the rainbow. It had colors and was beautiful. I was very happy because I saw the beautiful rainbow.

We were interrupted by a deaf student who requested Dr. McKinney's presence at the Christmas party. I made a tentative appointment for after the new year when I could observe classes and continue the interview. I said I would write her after the new semester had begun. "I'm too busy to write back, but yes, come back and visit when it's not so hectic," she half signed and said, and invited me to spend the day observing classes. "But before you visit again, you must read my dissertation. It would be a waste of time to repeat and explain everything to you. Call me after you've read my dissertation."

I thanked her and left the building to face Friday's rush-hour traffic in downtown Los Angeles. I wanted to drive immediately to Claremont Graduate School and find the dissertation. Monday seemed weeks away.

It finally arrived, and I almost got a speeding ticket on Interstate 10 in my haste to read the story of Joe which would validate what I had experienced with Ildefonso and prove what I knew intuitively, that Ildefonso was not a freak. In the stacks I found *First Language Learning in Deaf Persons Beyond the Critical Period.* The plain black-covered dissertation looked like every other dissertation on the shelf, but I carried it carefully, like a Gutenberg Bible, to the nearest table. I opened the cover slowly, still catching my breath from running up two flights of stairs to the stacks. After skimming through two thirds of the pages, I found Joe.

When Joe first began his education at about age eighteen, he did not communicate with any signs or even gestures. He shrugged and put his palms up in response to any gestures, signs, or speech directed at him. Like Ildefonso, Joe seemed to studiously note events and interactions around him, but did not know how to join or interpret them.

Both Ildefonso and Joe had had to figure out enough about the world to fend for themselves. Both lived outside of society, but unlike Ildefonso, Joe didn't have even minimal support from his family. There was no uncle to provide a name, birthdate, and some history. After learning a few signs and gestures, Joe had managed to ask for help by gesturing that he didn't work and had no money and no place to live. Whenever he saw someone sleeping on the street he would point to himself and nod. He was even more alone than Ildefonso, and the world treated him as less than human. He didn't have enough data attached to his person to be acknowledged. Since he had no name and no language to explain where he was born, he was given no rights to exist where he was found.

Joe not only had no idea where he was from, but like Ildefonso he knew nothing of geography or political boundaries. A map meant nothing to him and was met with his characteristic shrug. McKinney describes how Joe became upset once about pieces of paper and their importance. After pointing to some papers, he mimed writing on one and threw it across the table.

Joe and Ildefonso reacted differently to their first use of language. Whereas Ildefonso wanted everything explained and asked questions more frequently than he tried to express his own thoughts, Joe as soon as he learned a few signs wanted to tell about himself and explain things. Aside from this personality difference, their language-learning experiences were remarkably similar.

Joe, like Ildefonso with his "green," expected a single sign to communicate magically all that he associated with that new symbol. McKinney describes Joe's attempt to communicate some important information using a gesture first and then its sign replacement. First he used to point to the refrigerator, shiver, and wait for a response. Frustrated by any subsequent simple explanation about coldness or cold things, he frowned, threw up his hands and ended the communication. After he learned the sign for cold, he used it with the same look of expectation as he had the gesture. After thinking for a while, he signed "cold" again and mimed putting on coats, pairs of pants, and knee-high boots, and signed "cold" again.

Gradually, as Joe learned language, Dr. McKinney understood that "cold" connoted his home or wherever he was from. Pictures of cold places were brought out for him to inspect. He said the trees were too small or somehow wrong in the pictures of California mountains. The trees were the right size in the pictures of Alaska, and Joe was pleased, pointing and nodding to what was probably his home.

To these two languageless men, "green" and "cold"

conveyed not simple stories but whole autobiographies. Ildefonso and Joe wanted and needed to communicate who they were. Both of them understood that people were asking for information about themselves, even though they didn't understand the questions. Without any way of referring to the past, they held their pasts inside of themselves. When finally given some basic tools, they anxiously began expressing their personal histories. They excitedly experimented with the new faster method of pointing—a sign or a word—and both were frustrated when this new magic failed to transmit their stories.

Meeting and studying Joe triggered another hundred questions in me. It also elicited a strong desire to find Ildefonso. When he and I parted, Ildefonso was only four months old in language, less than a year old when I saw him last. By now he should have learned enough language to answer some of my old and new questions in detail. I went to the registry of interpreters where I used to work and asked if anyone knew Ildefonso. All the faces were new to me, and no one had heard of anyone by that name. I asked after Elena, LuAnn, Juanita, and as many students as I could remember, but with no success. If Ildefonso had gone back to Mexico, I would never be able to find him. I called as many people as I could and collected a page of names and phone numbers of interpreters and teachers before returning home.

During the second week of January, I wrote to Dr. McKinney, thanking her again for meeting with me and suggesting a time for my second visit. During a follow-up phone call she agreed to the time and with some hesitation said that I could probably look at some of her files. When I arrived, she and I spoke for a few minutes before I observed classes for a couple of hours. I headed straight for the beginning class and watched a young teacher, Erika, help five students fill out a standard form. They needed to be able to write their names, birthdates, addresses, and the date in the right spaces. While they worked alone for a few minutes, Erika gave me the history of each student.

Four out of the five were foreign-born and had been prelingual adults. José, from Central America, communicated with his family with a basic set of gestures. He knew the alphabet, but no words. From October to March of that year, he had copied signs and words but grasped no meaning behind them. Just two weeks before, his mind had opened. Suddenly the moment of understanding, of revelation, came, and he realized that the symbol, whether a sign or a word, carried something bigger than itself. As with Ildefonso, this insight flashed like a vision.

"Why do you think José took so long to realize language?" I asked Erika. She thought that the number of students in the group might have been a factor. Perhaps individual tutoring would have speeded up his learning. Also, she began teaching in signed English, using her voice while she signed. She noticed that José began to mix up English and ASL. His signs made no sense. She saw him sign "do," meaning *action* or *activity* in ASL, when he was asked to make a question out of a statement. He had learned the sign, "do," from her signed English questions, such as, *Do you want the book?* Whenever he saw a question mark on the board, he signed "do." Erika corrected her mistake and began signing ASL without mouthing any words. José's signs began to make more sense, and soon he saw language.

She went on to describe other foreign students who all began without language. All experienced the language revelation within six months after their first lesson except her fourth languageless student, who still memorized and copied without understanding. She labeled him "environmentally retarded." He lacked the interactions and experiences that Joe, Ildefonso, and her other students had. In protecting him, his family had done his thinking for him.

In Erika's four years of teaching, she had met about fifteen languageless adults. Most of them worked at least six months before the awareness of meaning occurred— before the light bulb flashed. Once again I felt an overwhelming pull to find Ildefonso and ask him questions about his past, including any exposure to language teaching before me. I had concentrated on Ildefonso alone during our lessons, and our first week was intense, whereas Erika had never had the luxury of just one student. Even so, compared to six months, how unlikely one week seemed before the sense of language hit.

I began to write down all the questions I must ask Ildefonso if I could find him. Seeing him sign would be enough to answer questions about his progress after I had gone, I thought as I noticed one of the formerly prelingual students signing a complex sentence. I turned to leave after firmly fixing the picture of that class in my head: four signing students who all would have sat like motionless, speechless statues just one or two years earlier.

Don Briedenthal's class was the next level these students would enter. I visited there next, because the students were still beginners and some might have been without language recently. Don's students represented many parts of the globe: Cambodia, Nigeria, Iran, Lebanon, Ecuador, and Mexico. They appeared quite lively and frequently interrupted the teacher to interject a question or a comment. Some signed quite well, and one awkwardly but not shyly. Don used humor and a variety of explanations and examples to teach the English *follows* as in "January follows December." I had never thought about it before, but that is confusing. When these visually-thinking students looked at the calendar, they saw that January definitely comes after December and doesn't follow, in the sense of being behind. The students enjoyed making fun of English speakers but finally accepted the idea and practiced a few sentences. They definitely had fun in class and consequently learned a great deal.

While the students wrote sentences, Don discussed his class with me and told me a few of his experiences. The student who had the most trouble with signs had been recently languageless and was just now learning English in addition to ASL. One day Don tested the class on their comprehension of recently taught signs. Most of the class knew enough basic English vocabulary to write the definition of the sign in English. The least educated student knew no English. He turned in his paper with a series of pictures that described the meanings of the signs. The cleverest cartoon was in response to the sign "recently." The first frame depicted a car accident and a witness standing by. The next frame showed the witness running to tell someone, followed by the person describing the accident, then pointing over his shoulder and signing "recently." Every cartoon managed to show his understanding of the sign presented.

The end of Don's class ushered in the morning break.

I followed him to the kitchen, which doubled as the staff lounge, where I met and informally interviewed the other teachers. Almost everyone had stories about teaching a prelingual adult. Those who taught the more advanced classes were involved not in the primary exposure to language but in the second or third year.

How could such a gulf exist between the universities and the streets? How could a researcher consider a prelingual deaf adult learning language a once-in-a-lifetime happening when four were sitting at the same table only a few miles away? I remember a social worker sharing her frustrations once about child-abuse victims. She saw case after case, even murder, for decades before society accepted the fact that it had a problem. In our modern world of fast communication, there are still vital links missing. Unfortunately, ivory tower is not an obsolete metaphor.

Dr. McKinney's assistant entered the kitchen, looked at me but announced to everyone, "Dr. McKinney would like to see you in her office." I followed him out. As I entered the smoke-filled room, Dr. McKinney waved her left hand in the direction of the only empty chair.

"I thought you were in a graduate program," she said at once, explaining that she had no idea I was writing on my own, although I had never indicated otherwise in our four months of communication.

I explained that I had become interested in writing something, at least an article or two, when I discovered how little had been written. Since people in university settings seemed ignorant of languagelessness, I thought it more productive to stay outside of academic circles. She agreed about the academic perspective but counseled me to go through the system in order to change it. She would not help me, she continued, now that she realized that I was not affiliated with a university. "Why should I help you with your commercial enterprise?" she asked.

I sat speechless, trying to understand how my interest could be interpreted as a commercial enterprise. Carefully, I explained that my curiosity and interest developed during and after my work with Ildefonso. I repeated how delighted I was to meet her and observe her program. She had more information than perhaps anyone in the United States on the language acquisition of deaf adults. The world, according to the card catalogs and the people I had met, was ignorant and needed this information. She had far more expertise and experience than I, and I would be more than happy to assist her. It would be far better for her to publish the information.

"I haven't the time. There is too much to be done here," she sighed, and lit another cigarette. She explained how difficult it was to get grants and contributions to keep the center open. She would probably have to lay off some of the faculty in the fall. I repeated my offer to help her. I could organize the information in her files, count the number of people that had learned their first language through her program, and note their progress. She could supervise, and she could publish.

I don't think she paid any attention. She didn't want to show me any of her files and concluded with, "If you were in a Ph.D. program, I'd help you because then I'd know you would be a future colleague." She had work to do; I was no longer welcome. I stared at the filing cabinet where lay clues about many once languageless minds, now closed, locked, and guarded by this woman and her clouds of smoke.

14

CHAPTER

■ ■ ■

THOROUGHLY DISCOURAGED after my dismissal by Dr. McKinney, I decided to write down my memories of Ildefonso, to retrieve all of our first conversations and relive the experience. I had written only two pages when a friend showed me a newspaper article about Dr. Oliver Sacks's new interest in the Deaf signing community. I had recently read his book *The Man Who Mistook His Wife for a Hat* and been impressed by his refreshing curiosity and humane interest in people. He reminded me of the scientist one sees in a five-year-old, curious about everything—all the details—and questioning everything, including his own previous assumptions and learning. I was delighted that this man was now looking at signed language and Deaf people. I wrote to him immediately and volunteered to interpret for him if he would like me to introduce him to some interesting Deaf people I knew. I also mentioned Ildefonso and my work with him. Dr. Sacks wrote back and wanted to know more about Ildefonso. I told him, and he gave the same response Ildefonso had after his first history lesson: "People need to know about this."

Reinvigorated, I decided to try another library and

visit the last century when, according to the graduate student I had seen, people were interested in language-lessness. While I found nothing about languageless deaf adults, I found a great many stories about wild children, and references to more. The stories covered children who survived alone in the wilderness, children adopted by animals, and children abused or imprisoned. One author added Helen Keller to the list because she grew so wild after becoming deaf and blind that her parents could not communicate with her enough to educate or control her.

I decided to study the wild-child stories to see how these languageless humans related to Ildefonso and the languageless deaf adults I had met. Many conclusions and beliefs I had read about the inability to learn language late in life were derived from the study of wild children.

A boy in Germany, Kaspar Hauser, lived in a dark room from infancy to age seventeen. A man fed him but never communicated with him or even let himself be seen. Kaspar, after appearing in Nuremberg in 1828, learned some language, speech, and social conventions. He began to explore the world, and although he remained emotionally stunted, he progressed rapidly from his in-fantile state. He began to recall his life in darkness. This must have scared whoever had kept him, for Kaspar was murdered only five years after he was released from his prison.

A recent technical account of an unsocialized child, *Genie: A Psycholinguistic Study of a Modern Day "Wild Child,"* is about a girl whose psychotic father tied her to a chair from infancy to adolescence. Susan Curtiss, the author, describes the child's limited progress during re-habilitation. Genie learned some language, but did not progress beyond the stage of a four- or five-year-old.

Perhaps the most famous story is the one that captured attention during the time of great debates and discussions about the nature of man and the noble savage. The child who generated the most interest, both at the time and up to the present, was known as the wild boy of Aveyron. François Truffaut's film *L'Enfant sauvage* is a moving documentary about this twelve-year-old boy who wandered out of the woods into a French village in January 1800.

Roger Shattuck in his narrative about the same boy, who was later known as Victor, describes the excitement in Paris at the idea of a subject who could provide the answer to the many questions concerning the true nature of human beings. Studying the biological and natural state of a human is impossible, because of the immediate influence of socialization and education. The only way to separate the biological creature from the social is to separate a child from society at or soon after birth. Obvious moral problems make this unthinkable, but by abandoning Victor, his parents performed the forbidden experiment (the phrase Shattuck takes as the title of his book). The new French republic and the newly formed Society of Observers of Man took advantage of the opportunity, and Victor became the property of the state.

Victor could not speak, did not respond to human speech, did not control any of his bodily functions, and preferred nakedness to clothing even in winter. Indeed, he seemed not to notice temperature extremes. He walked barefoot in snow and grabbed potatoes from burning coals with bare hands, eating them before they cooled. He often tried to escape from his human captors.

Many involved themselves in the study or training of Victor at the beginning, but eventually his care and education fell into the hands of Doctor Jean-Marc Itard, an ambitious physician, and Madame Guérin, the house-keeper at the National Institution for Deaf-Mutes in Paris. In his book, Shattuck looks at not only Victor's entry into society, but the reactions of different people to Victor. Some found him useful as a scientific subject and abandoned him when he no longer served their pur-poses. Some responded to his wildness with immediate training efforts to socialize him, to make him "human." Some saw him as a hopeless case and advocated a life sentence in an institution for the mentally ill and defec-tive. Only a few, Madame Guérin being the most notable example, offered him acceptance and human warmth. Vic-tor lived with Madame Guérin for twenty-two years, after Itard and others turned to new experiments and other interests. Shattuck's observations include reactions of people today. He notes:

> When adults hear about the case of the Wild Child, they usually ask how he turned out. They want to know . . . if he grew up to live some kind of useful and happy life. Children, when told about the boy, ask what he was really like and, above all, how he managed to live in the woods all by himself. . . . But they often ask another, more searching question: What right did anyone have to capture him?

These different responses reminded me of my own mixed reactions upon meeting Ildefonso and his languageless world. On the one hand, I immediately wanted to teach him language and make him a part of my world, assuming that this was the path to a "useful and happy life." On the other hand, I admired him for his ability to survive and create a life for himself, recognized the uniqueness of his languageless thoughts and perspective, and wondered about my right to try to change him to be more like me, especially if I failed and communicated to him only that he was deficient in some way. Education may always include the message that the student needs to become more like the teacher, thereby implying that the student or the student's thinking is inferior.

Shattuck recognizes the moral dilemma and the possibility of breaking Victor's spirit by education. Throughout his book, he wonders about the boy's perspective and reactions. In contrast, Harlan Lane and Richard Pillard, writing about a later wild child in *The Wild Boy of Burundi,* express a very different attitude. In response to letters asking about the moral implications of capturing and civilizing the alleged wild boy, Dr. Lane replies:

> I am saddened by the letters. What a grim commentary on our lives! Is life in the home sweet home so punitive that we prefer life in isolation, scrabbling for food, fleeing predators, neither giving nor receiving love? . . . With proper observation, John [the boy in Burundi], like Victor, can clarify what is characteristic about man, . . . Romulus and Remus, the satyrs in Greek and Roman antiquity and the Middle Ages, wild children in the Renaissance, Robinson Crusoe, Mowgli, Tarzan—for that matter, King Kong—all cry out for explanation. Perhaps John can help us to penetrate that mystery, too!

Later, Dr. Pillard describes some of their interactions with John:

The cavernous room is dimly lit. . . . It is oppressively hot and close. . . . We have sedated John with a 10 mg. shot of Valium, but he is in no mood to be X-rayed. He writhes, screams and flails when we try to position him on the table. . . . —the left leg! Hold him. You two take the right. You two take his shoulders (Harlan and I took his head). Now go! We quickly get six films. It is possible to overpower a ten-year-old boy; it's a question of numbers.

. . . I would dearly have loved to [knock him out]. I had had it with the day-long battle.

And later, he explains to the reader:

It was not easy for us to say goodbye to Deo [one of their hosts]; . . . and we would see Alan [a colleague] in a year's time. . . . Lastly, there was [John]. But at that moment he didn't enter our minds. If you think that is strange or hardhearted, you must try to understand the difference between caring for a friend and caring for a patient. . . . Two basically different postures are called for—one subjective, the other objective. Deo and Alan had become our friends and we were sorry to separate; it left us feeling incomplete. [John] was our patient and our puzzle; we had done what we could for and with him; we felt complete.

Itard, Victor's teacher, reacted to the puzzle that a wild boy presented and showed interest in Victor's training as a scientific experiment, but he also demonstrated affection for the boy. "After his fashion," Shattuck writes,

Itard the scientist was 'in love' with this rude creature, whom he wanted to mold into a man after his own image. . . . There is something as touching and as outrageous as Pygmalion's prayer and as Narcissus' desire for his reflection, something as audacious as Prometheus' theft of fire, symbol of creation. For Itard presumed to confer, if not life, at least intelligence and humanity.

Regardless of the specific response to wild children, whether empathetic, curious, or purely scientific, almost everyone reacts strongly. All of France turned to Victor when he first emerged from the woods. Peter, a wild boy from Hanover, became the talk of London after King George I took an interest in him, and he became the inspiration for the Yahoos in Jonathan Swift's *Gulliver's Travels*. People in this century as well as the last continue to be enthralled with Defoe's Man Friday, Burroughs's Tarzan, and Kipling's Mowgli, all of whom have inspired films.

But we are simultaneously attracted and repelled. We envy the freedom, yet we fear the wildness. Our animal qualities frighten us, and every culture spends considerable effort in denying or hiding certain aspects of our nature. The anthropologist Mary Douglas calls our means of dividing nature and culture the purity rule. Social conventions, communication, and language usage are determined and enforced through the purity rule. Physiological processes, common to all animals, are considered dirty. She points out, "To domesticate an animal means to teach it to bring organic processes under control. To socialise a child means the same thing." An animal-like child challenges our most sacred ideas of humanness. Thus, wild children are often treated horribly upon capture, with the intention of making them more "human."

Deaf people encounter similar reactions from the hearing world. People are repulsed by sounds that seem more animal-like than human. Often, even among parents, the inability to speak is associated with mental retardation. Ildefonso never made a sound. Only months after I met him did I hear a tiny sound—a high-pitched soft tone when he laughed. I'm sure he was quite capable of producing a great range of vocal noises, but he learned, as do most deaf people, how to avoid disapproving and even shocked looks from those around him. People often describe the vocalizations produced by deaf people as eerie, animalistic—inhuman. The frequent mistreatment of deaf persons may stem from the same fear as that provoked by wild children. If deaf children or adults are also languageless, they run a greater risk that their humanity will be denied.

Human beings gain a sense of security, false though it be, from conformity, from the lack of startling differences that would force us to contemplate who we really are. Like Snow White's witch, we don't want to face a mirror that tells the whole truth. But for the person who can look past the noises or wildness or strange gesturing and recognize the capabilities and potential of another human being, a gift awaits. Itard, Madame Guérin, and Helen Keller's teacher, Anne Sullivan, all learned about themselves through their wild children. As Shattuck writes, "Most of us live within the middle range of human experience, yet we need some knowledge of the further limits. These cases, especially those of extreme isolation and deprivation, are like special mirrors that reveal hidden parts of our own humanity and animality."

Itard and Anne Sullivan experienced their own kind

of awakening or revelation as they witnessed Victor's and Helen Keller's births into language: "At that moment," writes Shattuck, "something specifically human, something that links us all together, revealed itself more suddenly and dramatically than ever happens with a two-year-old infant. Helen grasped, simultaneously, the possibility of a code signifying our notions of things in the world and the meaning of the specific sign Anne was writing on her palm: water." The entrance to language is the entrance to the human family. No one is fully human alone.

Ildefonso shared with Victor, Kaspar, and Genie the experience of languagelessness and the consequent exclusion from the human community, but that similarity—indeed, a great one—is the only one. Deafness is not wildness, and the isolation of languagelessness alone is not the isolation of the woods or a basement or imprisonment on a chair. The differences between Victor and Ildefonso or Genie and Joe are more significant than their common languagelessness.

Almost completely isolated from human contact, not just language, wild Victor, abused Genie, and imprisoned Kaspar had severely limited experiences, which retarded their growth mentally, emotionally, and spiritually. They are very different from languageless deaf adults and do not serve well as studies on late language acquisition. We credit language with playing an enormous role in personality and moral development, mental health and intelligence, but the differences between Ildefonso and wild children challenge us to re-examine what gives us our human attributes.

Ildefonso had a sense of morality and expressed ideas and convictions about how people should live and treat others, while Victor seemed to lack any idea of right and wrong. He grabbed anything he wanted, oblivious to any idea of property. Ildefonso asked me about greed before he knew the sign, and saw it as aberrant behavior. He exhibited none of the egoism described in Victor.

In many ways, abused or abandoned children seem to lack awareness of self and of their relationship to others. Shattuck describes Victor by saying, "He had existed without being alive—alive to the fact and the miracle of his own life. . . . He had been deaf in the worst way of all. He couldn't hear himself; he couldn't hear himself living." Ildefonso knew he was human, in spite of not always being treated as such; he had a sense of self. One of the first characteristics that attracted me to him was his strong desire to relate to others, to communicate even without tools.

15

CHAPTER

■■■

WHILE READING ABOUT LANGUAGELESS Victor I became increasingly anxious to find Ildefonso. I had to see if he had continued to improve. I packed my VW Rabbit and drove over four hundred miles from the San Francisco Bay area to southern California. I searched out interpreters, Deaf friends, teachers, any signing resource I could find, and asked all of them if they knew of any language-teaching programs, rehabilitation counselors, or vocational-training programs that might be serving languageless deaf adults. Invariably, I had to explain that "languagelessness" meant lacking signed as well as spoken languages. Many Deaf people have inferred from hearing people's questions that their signing doesn't count as language. Deaf children, usually from Deaf families, with well-developed ASL are often described in school reports as having low-functioning language skills. What this means is that the teacher cannot read fluent signing. I also asked whomever I met associated with the Deaf community if he or she knew of Ildefonso or Elena or Juanita. Many interviews and hundreds of miles later Ildefonso still eluded me, but the trip proved immensely valuable, nonetheless.

I found Robyn Natwick, who had done a study comparing two adults who had learned ASL as their first language. She videotaped them and analyzed their individual and shared linguistic idiosyncrasies. I met some recently languageless students and their teachers, who shared stories about how their students had learned language and entered the human community.*

The next few phone calls and meetings directed me to an adult education center with a large program serving deaf students. Perhaps someone there might have news of Ildefonso. No one had, but I was directed to a class that reminded me of the class where I had met him. Nothing had changed in the ten years since. Before me was another group of almost illiterate, uneducated deaf adults, almost all of whom had spent their entire lives in an educational system.

I could understand how information is difficult or impossible for languageless people to receive, but I continued to be surprised when I met signing Deaf adults who remained ignorant of basic facts. After meeting some parents and caretakers of deaf children, I realized that part of the problem is overprotection. Parents, teachers, and professionals take too much responsibility, keeping deaf people from independence. I remembered seeing an interpreter in a college class screen the deaf students from the professor's off-color remarks and swearing by changing and deleting his words to tone down the profanity.

Jane Curtan, the teacher for the class I visited, ex-

---

* Some of these stories are included in the Afterword.

plained that her deaf students lacked the informal education that usually takes place in homes because of the communication barrier between them and their parents. She discovered that her students were bored by books, because they had no understanding of the purpose of writing—they had had no storytelling in their lives, except in ASL. She began telling them stories from books, for the sake of the stories themselves, without direct ties to any lesson, and introduced them to the library. She and the librarian gave them a tour of the subjects and stories found in books, and Jane referred them to books to find answers to their questions. They were astounded to find that the answers actually were in books, and a few of them began to visit the library on their own time.

In *Lessons in Laughter,* Bernard Bragg, a Deaf actor and storyteller, points to another reason for deaf people's lack of education:

> . . . the sad part is that such an enormous amount of time was and still is being spent on teaching deaf children how to speak and lipread adequately, and their speech remains harsh and unaccented to the ear of the hearing. Most of that time could have been spent more profitably on teaching them to read and write well. That is one reason why many deaf children are less literate than their hearing counterparts.

After a morning with Jane and her class, which included five languageless students, I called and tracked down several more signing acquaintances. None of them had heard of Ildefonso, but, "There's a Deaf man, L. Timmons, who teaches sign language at the Salvation Army. He might know," someone suggested. "He knows everyone."

I drove to the agency where Mr. Timmons worked. He didn't know Ildefonso, but he did know Elena and where she now taught. I thanked him and immediately called Elena's school. I was too late; all the teachers had left. I had to return to Northern California, but at least I had finally found a possible lead.

Reluctantly, I faced the eight hours of driving. I disliked the idea of driving hundreds of miles away from Ildefonso when I felt so close to finding him. Back in the San Francisco area, I continued collecting information about languageless people and their teachers. Someone told me about a program that worked specifically with languageless or low-functioning deaf adults in San Francisco. A few more phone calls put me in touch with Alice Nemon and Holly Elliott, two of the administrators of The Independent Living Skills Laboratory at San Francisco State University. During the short time that the program was funded, it helped at least twenty-five students begin to learn their first standard language. I could have listened to their language-acquisition stories for days, but first I had to find Ildefonso.

I finally reached Elena by telephone. She was very surprised to hear from me and asked where I'd been and what I'd been doing. I hurried through a brief summary of the past seven years, asked how she had been, listened, and finally got to the subject of Ildefonso. She had stayed in contact with him, knew where he lived and where he worked. He was now a gardener, but he didn't have a telephone, so she agreed to act as our liaison and work out where and when Ildefonso and I could meet. We set a time to plan the reunion after she checked Ildefonso's schedule. In the meantime, I asked her to give Ildefonso a present for his birthday, which was in the following week, along with my greetings and hopes to see him soon. I hung up the phone and paced excitedly for the next hour trying to imagine the new Ildefonso. Finally, I had found him. I wanted to call him immediately, but even if he had had a telephone, I had no teletype machine to make a long-distance conversation possible. I wondered if he knew enough English now to read and write tele-typed communications.

Some friends of mine from England invited me to spend Christmas with them in a house they had rented in a beautiful old orchard in Southern California not too far from Ildefonso. I called Elena and suggested we meet there. She readily agreed, and we set a time.

The day finally arrived, and I nervously helped pre-pare for the visit. I gave my friends a crash course in American Sign Language so that everyone could intro-duce themselves, greet the guests, and offer "more" of whatever they were eating. Michael, the host, specialized in visual questions, drawing big question marks with his arched brows and dotting them with big round eyes. But his mother, Violet, a retired school teacher, won the award for Best Facial Expressions. Over half of the dif-ficulty for beginning signers is matching their face's mes-sage to their signs.

I jumped to my feet when I heard a car in the drive-way and ran out the front door just as Ildefonso turned the corner into the garden. We both slowed down and shyly approached each other. Our greeting felt awkward and formal until we hugged. Hugs have a wonderful way of melting years. We couldn't stop smiling from our hug for the rest of the day.

My friends lined up and, like children performing their practiced Christmas lines, introduced themselves and fingerspelled their names: A-n-n-a, J-a-n, M-i-c-h-a-e-l, and V-i-o-l-e-t. To this day I don't think any of them know any other letters of the manual alphabet.

Before we had finished filling the living room, Ildefonso turned and scolded me for giving him a birthday present. I shouldn't have done that, he told me, and handed me a present of his own. "For Christmas," he said. I couldn't help remembering his first scolding concerning the burrito. I was not to give him more than he gave me. He wanted me to open it and looked worried while I did. The box contained fruit-scented soaps from England. I commented on how lovely the colors and fragrances were and thanked him. He beamed.

I couldn't identify my feelings as I watched Ildefonso sign with confident, fluid movements. At first I thought perhaps the swelling and tightness inside might be akin to parental feelings, but no, that wasn't right. We had struggled too much together, conspiring against something big and unknown. He, too, seemed uncertain about our relationship. Intermittently, he would begin a story as if to brag or show off to his teacher, but he always caught himself, and the remark became casual, as is appropriate between friends. So neither of us gave in to any outburst of emotion or spoke down or up to the other. Above all, we wanted to be friends.

Ildefonso asked about England, and my friends and I interpreted a few comments in answer until Elena picked up the conversation and began describing her trip there.

Since everyone was listening to her, Ildefonso began our first private conversation with, "I'm disappointed. When I heard your friends were from England, from so far away, I thought they would look different, but they look the same as all of you."

Then, as if he suddenly figured out why, he said, "The history lesson . . . ?" I nodded instantly. He didn't need to say more. "I remember that," he continued. "Whenever I can, I find an interpreter to interpret the television news. It's important to know what's happening in the world. I don't understand why there's so much killing and war and stealing, people arguing about who owns what all the time. I think it's because some people are greedy, and they want more than they need. I want some land and a place to live, but just a small place and a little land, so I can have my own garden. There is enough in the world for everyone to have a little garden. Everyone could be content. But some people want gigantic houses and gigantic gardens, so they fight and steal and buy up all the land and others can't have anything."

I was dumbfounded. What I couldn't have understood from him in four months, he had just expressed in less than two minutes. I tried to put the nameless, languageless man with the folded arms together with the confident living-room conversationalist. I agreed with what he said by nodding my head and signing "yes," but the only comment I could make was that his signing was now better than mine.

He looked at me emotionally and signed, "You— you knew me before." He re-enacted our first meeting, portraying himself as a helpless, ignorant fool, holding his hands in front of his face, making miniature nonsense

164

signs, and looking at them as if they were mysterious snakes. He straightened up and signed, "And now?" and mimed a composed intelligent signer. I had to gulp down my drink and hide behind my glass for a minute to control my rush of feeling.

"Your signing is wonderful," I managed to say.

"I'm still learning," he responded. "I want to learn more, but I'm tired in the evenings after work. Of course, I have learned many more words: t-r-e-e, c-a-r, j-o-b . . ." He looked around, pointed, and fingerspelled d-o-o-r. "I need to keep studying." I was amused and touched that he was trying so hard to be nonchalant, yet had to show me a few words as evidence of his studies.

"Do you remember when you asked me about apple picking?" Ildefonso asked. "That was in New York." He had understood my question, or worked it out later, but since he had no place names, he could not answer my "where" question. I had guessed Washington State, and he accepted my guess at the time. But he remembered not only the question but my wrong guess, even though at the time he didn't know Washington from India.

Michael interrupted to offer him a drink, which he refused, and explained that while he was with the apple-picking crew, he had learned to associate drinking alcohol with rowdy behavior and trouble with the police. He had decided then never to touch a drink, and only once had his friends convinced him to try. That was a few years ago. He finally gave in and drank his first margarita, but he hated the dizzying effect. "Again? Drink-alcohol again? Never, never," he concluded.

As we continued to talk, Ildefonso expressed great satisfaction with his life and told me about all the major events since we were last together. He was a legal resident now and had a wonderful job at a beautiful private hospital where he not only tended but created gardens. He began to tell me about one of his first, best assignments, then hesitated shyly, glancing at Elena. She picked up the cue and described Ildefonso's garden. He himself had searched for the perfect pebbles, stones, driftwood, and shells, brought them back to where he worked, and carefully arranged them around a palm tree, some shrubs, and a sundial. As Elena described his creation in ASL, Ildefonso could not suppress a very proud smile.

His garden was not simply a work of art and a job well done; it was proof that he belonged. He had entered the world as a new member of the tribe. He not only had legal status and an official job, he knew what legal meant and what his job title meant. He could not only create a garden, he could name it and the city, country, and planet that contained it.

I fought to keep myself from crying, then congratulated Ildefonso on his garden and promised to visit it soon. He signed that he would be very happy to show it to me and repeated that he enjoyed his job. After a pause, he added, "Except it's lonely. No one signs."

16

CHAPTER

∎∎∎

A COUPLE OF MONTHS LATER, I crossed half of California again to meet Ildefonso. In addition to seeing his garden, I wanted to ask him more about his past life and languageless thinking. I found him hard at work, and at first he didn't see me. He was carefully covering the roots of a plant. Even his peripheral vision couldn't pick up my arm waving. I had to jump over a small bench and touch him on the shoulder to get his attention. He started and stared at me.

"Where did you come from? Where? Where?"

"I had to come and see your rock garden. I still haven't seen it. Where is it?"

"Go through those double doors to the inner court-yard. You'll see it." He still looked stunned.

"I'll be right back," I signed quickly, and followed his directions. The original garden had contained a large palm tree, a few ferns, shrubs, and a sundial. He had meticulously laid white and tan stones around the sundial and from the sundial to the near edge of the garden where more stones were placed as a border. Across the stones he had placed abalone shells and pieces of driftwood.

What struck me was the order and symmetry. All his angles were right angles, both where the stone paths met and where he had arranged driftwood on the stones. The shells lay at regular intervals between other shells or driftwood.

I remembered an incident I had read in Dr. McKinney's dissertation, when Joe displayed almost a passion for what he considered right and orderly. He was preparing coffee for some reporters at his apartment and became upset when he realized there were no saucers for his cups. He had meticulously set the table, and everything looked fine, but he insisted that without saucers he could not serve the coffee. Finally he found some bowls to put under the cups and was satisfied. Harlan Lane in *The Wild Boy of Aveyron* also describes Victor's need for ritualistic order after he had become socialized.

When these isolated beings had no or little understanding of their environments, they could not even imagine order. After they had been exposed to information and explanations, order became a possibility for them. It must give one a tremendous feeling of personal power to begin to organize and control some aspect of the environment after experiencing chaos for so long.

As soon as I walked back through the double doors, Ildefonso stood up and faced me. "Wonderful," I signed from yelling distance. "It's beautiful." He smiled shyly and gave me a small "Thank you."

I began to ask my first question, but he interrupted me, signing, "Where, where did you go? Where?" I misunderstood at first and thought he was repeating his first question—where did I come from when I appeared so suddenly. I started to explain that I couldn't get his attention, but he interrupted me again, asking, "Where did you go? I saw you one day a long, long time ago and then you disappeared. Then you suddenly appear, and we meet again. Where were you all that time?"

So much had happened to me since I saw Ildefonso at the bus stop, I didn't know what to say. "The summer after I saw you," I began the brief history, "John and I moved across the country for his medical training and my graduate school. During the next two years, I lost my father and my husband. I moved back to the West Coast and began a new life. I thought of you often and finally had the chance to look for you."

"Your father?" Ildefonso asked.

"Yes, my father died," I answered. I noticed that he stared for a minute at the sign for "dead" or "to die." Then he nodded like a sympathetic friend or an old person who had heard similar stories many times before.

"And now? What are you doing? Where are you living?" Ildefonso asked.

I answered that I had moved to the San Francisco area and was writing the story about his amazing journey to language and his new life. It needed to be told, and I would like to continue writing it, although it would be exciting if he could do it himself someday. He smiled widely and began to explain that he needed to save enough money to be able to go to school (*enough* for Ildefonso and his culture does not mean until he is comfortable, but until his entire extended family is; as long as a brother or cousin or close friend needs help, he will work). He wanted to continue learning English, and he wanted to learn how to write, but it would take a long time. So I should write the story. He looked very pleased, although he had trouble believing that his experiences would be in a book. He could read hundreds, perhaps a thousand, isolated words, but his ASL grammar couldn't provide any clues on how to put English words together. The world of print was still a mystery to him.

I explained that after the story was finished I would have no control over where it went or who could read it. Anyone, even in another part of the world, could read it and find out about him. And I explained that I would make sure he would stay anonymous and keep his privacy. He liked that idea but looked astounded that it could be otherwise. I fingerspelled the pseudonym for his name that I was using, and he asked me to repeat it. "It's common in the area where you were born," I informed him.

He frowned, commenting, "That's a really funny name." I almost laughed. Here was a man who hadn't known that names existed for most of his life. I remembered the look of surprise when he first learned his name. And now he frowned and laughed at a new name. I wondered if all names still appeared a little funny to him.

"Ildefonso, could you help me?" I asked. "What did you think before language? What was your life like?"

Ildefonso answered without hesitation, beginning as if on cue: "I remember when I was very young, and I began noticing words on paper and in books. I didn't know what they were, but I was curious. One day I saw children with books walking down the street. They were my height, and I knew they were going to learn what was in those books. I pointed to the children and begged my parents to let me go with them, to send me where they were going." The last sentence Ildefonso mimed, acting out the way he had communicated with his parents. He dropped to his knees and put up his hands in a prayer sign—a scene he must have seen many times in the Catholic church. He signed "please" at first, but in his mime changed it to an imploring face.

"Please, please, I want to study books. I want to go to school. Please," he signed to me what he could not say in word or sign to his parents. "With words I could learn what's in books, learn how to drive, learn mathematics and science," he explained, still pleading with me as if practicing for a second chance with his parents, now that he could articulate his desire. "My parents refused and wouldn't send me to school. They told me I was a 'dummy' (a derogatory sign referring to deaf people) and could not learn." He showed no anger or resentment, but explained that his parents were very poor and needed him to work. Work, I remembered, included begging when he was still quite young.

He didn't really answer the question of what or how he thought, but he needed to tell me this story. He wanted to tell me and later the readers of my book that although he was ignorant, he had always had a desire to learn. Several times then and later, I repeated my question of how or what he thought, but he always answered by describing what had happened to him and why he remained uneducated. I sensed some embarrassment or the same self-blame that he had expressed years before with "dumb me." He considered it more important to communicate the frustration and darkness in his life than what he thought. And he probably couldn't imagine anyone being interested in his languageless state.

At the time he begged for education, he had no idea what was in those books, but now he chose mathematics and science as examples of what he could have learned. I wondered if what little he had learned about science matched his child's image of the keys that waited in words and books, keys that could unlock the mysteries all around him. If he had been born nearer to language and more resources, that curious intelligent boy might easily be a scientist now instead of a gardener.

Ildefonso began telling me news about our only mutual friend, Elena. "When did this happen?" I asked at one point, curious to see how he now talked of time. Ildefonso looked up above my right ear, thinking. "When?" I persisted. "Weeks ago? Months ago?"

"A while back," he said, using the general past tense sign. "Wait. . . . Christmas, yes, about three weeks after Christmas, after I saw you," he recalled suddenly. So Ildefonso knew how to talk about time, but counting time was still a foreign idea. He always had to take a cultural leap.

"I don't want to keep you from your work, but could I ask one more quick question?" Ildefonso nodded. "Before you met me, did anyone else teach you?"

"I was in a class right before I met you, but I never knew what was going on. I just sat and watched everyone signing and working." I knew Ildefonso's observant mind must have absorbed much, and I suspected that his unconscious had incubated information that contributed to his later revelation about language.

"Let's have dinner together sometime this week, and we'll have more time to talk, OK?" I suggested.

"Yes, Tuesday is a good day for me," he signed with ease. "Here's my address. We can meet there. I'll see if my brother, Mario, can come. He's in town now and just got a job this week."

"Of course, good. What time?" I asked, very conscious of how much and how fast we could now communicate.

Ildefonso blew a puff of air through his lips, shrugged his shoulders, and signed, "It doesn't matter."

"What about six, then?" Another shrug. I wondered if his indifference to the clock came from his former ignorance or if we were simply repeating a typical Anglo-Mexican dialogue. I remembered wondering whether Ildefonso would stay like Ishi or change after language. I was glad that he hadn't completely conformed.

Ildefonso carefully explained that he could not hear me knocking at the door. "I'm deaf—I can't hear," he said very seriously, and told me that he kept the door unlocked—I should just walk in. At first I was surprised by the number of obvious details he gave me, but a second later I realized how recently he had learned exactly what made him different from others. Deafness and hearing were impossible concepts to explain when we worked together.

I said good-bye after apologizing for some of my rusty signing.

"No, your signing is good," Ildefonso responded. "I understand you better than some of my Deaf friends. They use too much English and fingerspelling, and I can't understand them." He thanked me for stopping by, apologized for not being able to hug me, pointing to his dirt-covered clothes, and returned to his plant.

That evening I became more and more excited about my recent talks with Ildefonso. We could converse easily and quickly, but our two meetings had been too short to answer most of my questions. My curiosity was tired of being put on hold. I called Elena, who had now been friends with Ildefonso for some time, and asked her a few questions about Ildefonso's past.

Starting at five or six, Ildefonso had helped to herd sheep and goats, plant and harvest sugar cane, and, as he had told me in mime, begged. At the age of about ten, his parents sent him to Mexico City to live with his grandparents. There he did any odd job he could find and begged when he found nothing. His two best jobs were slaughtering chickens and working on airplane parts.

I asked her if she had met Ildefonso's brother. She had. Mario had also been born deaf, she told me, and had never learned language. He still used a primitive system of gestures. This was a revelation. I had no idea that Ildefonso had had a deaf companion in his childhood. They must have developed their own signs. To meet him would be like meeting two Ildefonsos—before and after language. I invited Elena to join us for dinner. She accepted, and suggested a better meeting place than Ildefonso's apartment. She would tell Ildefonso and Mario and meet me at six-thirty Tuesday night.

On Tuesday I waited anxiously at the busy intersection, wondering if I were dreaming. Ildefonso's integrated personality and quickness no longer seemed as much of a miracle. Sharing some form of communication and friendship with a like person could make all the difference between yielding to despair and entertaining hope.

Elena emerged from a car in the nearest parking lot. We talked of languagelessness and Ildefonso's changed life while we waited for Ildefonso and Mario. I asked if Ildefonso tended to forget vocabulary that he didn't use frequently, and mentioned the way he stared at the sign "to die/dead."

"He forgets signs once in a while and needs to be reminded of their meaning, but 'dead' or 'to die' he probably didn't recognize right away because he prefers his own gesture." She showed me, and I had to agree it was an improvement, very poetic. She began to tell me about the gestural system, but then she saw Ildefonso's car turn the corner. We walked in that direction.

Soon the two men came toward us, both smiling. While Ildefonso strode purposefully and slowly, Mario strolled lightly, with a carefree gait. He was obviously the younger brother, teasing Ildefonso with his frequent impish grin. He hugged Elena and looked at me shyly. Ildefonso and I hugged hello, and Elena introduced me to Mario, using a strange sign I didn't understand. Later I figured out it was their sign for friend. No names were exchanged. We shook hands.

Names meant nothing to Mario, as they had meant nothing to Ildefonso when I met him. Ildefonso read my thoughts and decided to teach Mario his namesign. Mario looked bewildered and turned to Elena. She pointed to each person and signed each name, including his. She signed hers on her cheek as I did mine, but with a different movement and shape. Then she showed Mario his namesign and Ildefonso's. She repeated the signs once more, and Mario nodded his head. Ildefonso turned to him and asked if he understood by bringing his hands and chin up and frowning at his brother. Mario nodded affirmatively, but Ildefonso wanted evidence. Ildefonso pointed to everyone in turn, turned to Mario, and demanded a response. Mario pointed to Ildefonso and called him "Mario," then shrugged his shoulders, implying he forgot the rest. "No, no," Ildefonso said, using the common

Mexican gesture of wagging the index finger side to side.
"Mario—you." Ildefonso insisted on repeating the lesson,
but Mario only grinned at his demanding brother and
shrugged his shoulders a few times.

Elena asked Mario about his new job, using mime
and some strange signs. I understood most of the conversation because at least 80 percent was mime. Mario
described opening a door, rubbed his arms as if freezing,
and mimed stacking cartons or pies or something flat onto
shelves while he shivered. Ildefonso looked from Mario
to me and whenever he caught my eye he would ask, "Do
you understand?" and smile smugly.

Elena asked what kind of food Ildefonso wanted:
Mexican? Chinese? Italian? Ildefonso shrugged and said
it didn't matter. Mario looked confused. He didn't understand any of the signs. Elena began to describe the
different foods, but Ildefonso interrupted. He could see
that Mario didn't understand the descriptions. He told
her what kind of food Mario liked. They decided he might
like to try Vietnamese food. Elena pointed to her mouth,
then down the street, and Mario and the rest of us followed her.

The restaurant looked exotic and elegant, with white
linen, mirrored walls, hanging vines, and fresh flowers
everywhere. A waiter in a starched white jacket seated
us and handed everyone a large menu. Mario and Ildefonso stared at their menus, pretending to read until the
waiter left the room. Elena described different dishes to
Mario in mime, with occasional help from Ildefonso.
Mario motioned that she should decide.

Ildefonso sat across from me and next to Mario. He
signed to me, "Watch this; it's really different." He turned
to Mario and ordered him to start gesturing so I could

see what it looked like. Mario didn't understand that Ildefonso wanted him to start a conversation. He kept trying to figure out what Ildefonso's conversation was about. "Later, you'll see," Ildefonso assured me.

The food came. After Mario had served himself and begun eating, Ildefonso told me that this was the first Vietnamese food his brother had ever eaten. "He's never tasted food like this—never," he explained. The sentence delighted me, because I had once given up trying to teach Ildefonso what *never* meant and how to use it. It had seemed an impossible concept. "My brother hasn't had a job," he continued, "so he's not used to these pleasures." Ildefonso seemed proud and happy to have his brother in town, so he could show him "these pleasures" and his new life.

I turned to watch Elena and Mario. As I studied their gestural conversation, I could tell Ildefonso was studying me. He looked from their conversation to me and constantly checked to see if I needed anything interpreted. Mario described a time when someone gave him some marijuana. To show the results, he squeezed his head while crossing his eyes and sticking out his tongue. Then he moved his hands, still in the shape of his head, and mashed the imaginary head while shaking his own.

The subject changed, and I picked up something about a child. I thought I saw Mario putting imaginary rings on. He was either saying that he was married or perhaps referring to his wife. I interrupted and asked, in mime, if he had children. Mario grinned broadly, either glad of the opportunity to share his good news or happy that he had understood my sign/mime communication. He held up three fingers and widened his smile. Elena had a picture of the oldest. He looked exactly like Ildefonso. Even Mario agreed. They were handsome children, and I signed "beautiful," which Mario seemed to understand. He nodded enthusiastically. I asked him if I could have one. He shook his head with a definite, "No." I signed "share." He immediately looked at Ildefonso, so I explained the sign by holding up three fingers with my left hand. With my right I patted the tops of three small heads and pointed to my fingers. I gave one finger-child to Elena, one to him, and kept one for myself. "Share," I repeated. He laughed and protested. Holding his hands over his heart he stooped over and showed a pained and saddened face. Immediately, he laughed and returned to his proud smile.

Ildefonso looked like a director constantly checking on each actor, studying every face. He translated for me and explained to his brother. Every two minutes he asked me if I had caught that gesture or noticed that sign. He also wanted me to note how differently we communicated than his brother.

Mario was telling a joke. I didn't understand much, but he actually ended with an almost coherent sound. All through dinner, Mario had admired Ildefonso for his communication skills, but now Ildefonso looked respectfully at his brother after he understood what Elena and I had heard. Ildefonso explained that Mario understood how to make sounds by copying mouth movements and making vibrations. Ildefonso had practiced for a while, but he could never make more than a couple of sounds. "Mario's pretty good at it," Ildefonso said proudly. To the two of them, especially Mario, this gift meant nothing more than any good parlor trick.

Elena asked Mario if he wanted sugar in his tea. He didn't understand. Ildefonso held his fist to the side of his mouth as if holding a stick and gnawed at the air with his teeth. Mario nodded instantly and looked at the sugar. Ildefonso explained that they had worked together picking sugar cane when they were young and used to chew on it during breaks. Their way of eating sugar cane became their common sign for sugar.

Ildefonso complained to Elena that I was not getting the full and complete picture of how they used to communicate. "This isn't right," he said. "She's not seeing it."

The waiter came with the bill, and Elena insisted on treating. Ildefonso signed "Thank you," nudged Mario and signed "Thank you" again slowly, toward Elena but looking at Mario. Mario stared blankly at Ildefonso. I remembered that look well. Ildefonso tried again. Mario pointed to his head and showed that there was only a little cube inside. He expanded his little cube a bit and gestured away and out from him (did this mean, "maybe in the future"?) and expanded the little brain some more. Finally, he shrugged his shoulders and raised his arms apologetically to Ildefonso. Ildefonso frowned an older-brother frown but accepted his excuse for the time.

He then turned to Elena and repeated his earlier complaint. He really wanted me to see the equivalent of a video showing Ildefonso and Mario growing up. He turned to me and apologized, explaining he could no longer gesture and mime with his brother the way he used to. He knew too much ASL. Language had changed him and his thinking.

"Could you drive us to see——?" Ildefonso asked Elena. I didn't catch the next sign, but before I knew it we were on a freeway to see someone, or something, I didn't know what.

Elena drove behind a restaurant, and we followed

Ildefonso to the back door by the garbage cans. He walked in while we waited. Soon he came out with a young man in an apron, who waved hello to us. "Watch, look at this," Ildefonso said to me, and began making gesture motions at the young man. The man looked at Ildefonso, then at Mario, then back at Ildefonso. "Come on, say something," Ildefonso ordered, a difficult performance in mime. The young man didn't understand, and Ildefonso nodded good-bye and walked quickly to the car. He wanted me to see languageless communication. It was very important to him to show me his old gestural state.

In the car, Ildefonso signed something to Elena from the back seat in the rearview mirror. Sitting in the front, I missed it. One minute later I noticed we were heading away from the restaurant where our cars waited. We stopped and began walking through a neighborhood with many small houses set close together. Ildefonso explained to me that he wanted to see if some of his friends were home. He wanted me to meet them. I followed him around the side of a house to a stream of light coming from an open door. A man appeared in the doorway when he saw our group approaching. He recognized Ildefonso and smiled back into the room while pointing out the door. Three faces peered out and greeted us. They knew everyone but me, and stared at me apprehensively. Elena introduced me as a friend, using the same sign I had seen in the parking lot. We all crowded into a small room, which contained three single beds. By the time I sat on the middle bed next to Elena, I felt stunned. I was sitting in the middle of a room full of languageless people.

17

■ ■ ■

I WATCHED MESMERIZED as they communicated for hours in mime. To the right of Elena was a middle-aged man of slight build with wiry arms that had grown strong from years of hard labor and skin that was leathery from decades in the sun and wind. The others seemed to defer to him, and the fact that he sat in the only chair appeared to be evidence of their respect. On the bed closest to the door sat the youngest, who could have been in his twenties but looked like a teenager. His bright eyes looked out from a smooth boyish face. To his right stood Mario with his almost permanent grin. Between Mario and me was Ildefonso, looking like an umpire, surveying every player and checking every interaction meticulously.

With some help from Elena and Ildefonso, I was able to figure out the few standard signs the men in the room had developed. In the course of that evening, they used only about a dozen common signs. Every other gesture was either a spontaneous invention or used by only one individual. Any sign that became adopted by the entire group had to be repeated and tested in many different stories and tried by everyone. If they could not achieve total consensus, the sign was dropped or remained the property of one person. I saw no common grammar or structure, but individuals developed their own systems for communicating ideas. Although the group may have understood an idea or a sign, it was never copied by anyone else. The young man used a forward rolling sign and then the same shape and movement backward, which I thought might suggest future and past, but my translation didn't quite work. Later, I realized that it didn't refer to time directly but acted as a fast-forward or reverse sign within the narrative. He wasn't saying "a little while later," but "moving ahead in the story."

I didn't dare blink, I was so afraid of missing something. I felt as if a time machine had flown me back to the Neanderthal Age, and I had the privilege of witnessing the invention of language. I consciously stuffed every gesture and interaction into my memory. Each movement was an experiment. Would it survive to become a permanent symbol, or would it die with this "conversation"? Would that rolling movement become the beginning of tense? The beginnings of the collective human mind emerged before me.

No one had a name. The introductions consisted of descriptions. The older man introduced the youngest with a story of how his mother had died while he was still a baby. In essence, his name was the description *the motherless one*. It reminded me of the *Iliad*. Names are secondary or incorporated into a description. Hera is not called "Hera," but "Hera with the white arms."

They told many border-crossing and border-patrol stories. The most breathtaking adventure involved a horse chase. The older man not only played himself running and sweating, but also played both the mounted officer and the horse. These people all lived on the edge, in constant fear of starvation. Their biggest challenge collectively and individually was figuring out how to stay on this side of the mysterious border, where jobs and food for their families existed. Each story contained a grain of information about how to enter white-man's land or avoid deportation. No one could say to another, "Guess what I found out. In order to cross or stay legally . . ." Instead, a story that contained some fact had to be told and retold until someone else either understood the significance or at least understood that the teller knew something important. Eventually, they all saw that little cards worked to repel green men. They showed me their collection. I think only one or two cards had any validity. The others were either inappropriate or out of date. All of them were treated like pieces of gold.

During one story about arrest and deportation, the storyteller turned to the youngest, who wrote on his forearm: 1986. No one, including himself, knew what that meant, but he had figured out that it worked as an answer to certain questions. He had three different years associated with three different events relating to border-crossings or arrests and proudly displayed his arm as a chalk board when the moment seemed right. Everyone showed great respect and admiration for his skill.

The same man seemed to have the best arithmetic skills; he had figured out addition. All of them could count but not as high and as fast as the youngest. They counted by holding their palms out and extending their fingers, then they pushed their hands slightly forward to indicate ten. They turned their hands around, palms facing in, and pushed forward for twenty, and so forth until the counter lost track. I asked the youngest how old he was. After Ildefonso's translation, he answered, "Ten-twenty-one."

"No, no, no," corrected Ildefonso. "Try again," he gestured.

"Ten-twenty-four, no, no, ten-twenty-five," he asserted without conviction. Ildefonso gave him the OK sign. I wondered whether Ildefonso had taught him that answer and if the man had any idea what he was counting.

Similarly, they all described the changing faces of the clock by counting out two pairs of numbers, ten-one, six. This meant 11:30. None of them knew hours and minutes or why 11:30 came twice a day, but they had managed to figure out when they had to be at work by memorizing the appropriate face of the clock. Numbers, a friend speculated after hearing this story, must be easier than other ideas, for we are all born with a dictionary for counting on our hands.

The men began to describe life in their Oaxaca villages. Different events and characters were acted out. One person started to describe someone or an incident as a way of saying, "remember when . . ." Another would have to repeat the story, adding a few details to prove that he understood the right reference. They complained of the worst jobs they had in Mexico. The older man hated plowing and began to describe oxen. Ildefonso interrupted and added a better description of oxen and the yoke, then let him finish his description. "Here, good," he signed by pointing to the ground, then giving the OK sign used by hearing people. He pointed to his back, aching under a plow, then repeated that it was better here on this side of the border.

I asked Ildefonso how many of the people came from the same village and how many in this circle of friends and relatives were deaf. Everyone watched Ildefonso in awe. His leap to language dumbfounded them. They didn't see language, of course, but they saw that he could communicate with outsiders, even people like Elena and me, who could talk without any hand movements. They considered him a genius and treated him with great respect. He had become the leader of the languageless clan. He addressed the group and asked how many people were like them in the village. He asked this by describing each person he could remember, including them, until someone understood and added one or two. They came up with about nine people, most of whom lived in or near the same village.

They had met at different ages and could not interact frequently or regularly due to their poverty and the constant need to work or find work. Even Ildefonso and his brother were separated, first by their age difference of about seven years and then by Ildefonso's various jobs. As a result, they had never had the chance to develop their gestural communication to the degree that some deaf siblings and children have. But what they lacked in standard vocabulary and structure, they tried to make up for in a tremendous variety of facial expressions and acting skills. Their repertoire of mimed stories seemed endless.

The youngest took the next turn on stage and began to describe his experience riding in an airplane. Everyone watched his story of the trip with an intense interest. Since even getting fed regularly is a problem for this group, a trip in an airplane is a rare adventure indeed. First the young man and his outstretched arms became the airplane taking off with bumping and rough vibrations. Then with his hand he showed the airplane becoming small and flying into the sky. Then as passenger he sat snugly in a chair, watching the world and its inhabitants shrink to toy size. He looked up and a woman stood waiting to serve him. He settled into the luxury of a king; the world at his feet and service at his side. Regardless of how many details and repetitions he added to his story, he never lost his fascinated audience for a moment. I could tell he would be applauded for the telling of this prize story for many years.

Later in the evening, the oldest described how his wife gave birth only to girls. He prayed and prayed for a boy, but the next baby was also a girl. He acted out a downcast and depressed man who went out with his drinking buddies for consolation. He mimed drinking and drinking until he was drunk. He straightened up at the end of the story, gave a mischievous smile, and laughed. He hadn't needed any language to pick up certain attitudes and behaviors in his culture, from the act of kneeling with hands together and pleading to drowning his sorrows in a bar.

Someone described traveling to the mountains and seeing white cold snow, an unimaginable substance to a native of southern Mexico. Another, specifically addressing me, described the time Elena ate a corn patty spiked with their favorite hot peppers. She had to drink a gallon of water. Everyone laughed with particular delight at remembering that incident. The stories went on and on, about their various jobs, a murder they witnessed, their funniest relatives, and always one more border-crossing incident.

Their ability to communicate without language astounded me. Telling stories from their similar histories and reminding each other of shared experiences were not trivial pastimes. Their mimed skits made them human, providing them with the only sense of community they could experience. Their storytelling was their main entertainment and education. Like the ancient Greeks telling and retelling the story of the Trojan war to keep their history and language alive, Ildefonso's friends repeated all of their stories to form their history and identity.

For a languageless tribe, repetition and audience participation are even more important than they were for the Greeks and are for present-day signing communities trying to preserve their language. This group is not passing on what is inherited; it is creating language. In order to understand one another, they all have to remember most of the details, especially chronology, for they can act only in the present tense. Each individual phrase or idiom is as important as the piece of information it carries, carefully examined by the storyteller and the audience together. The ostracized humans from Oaxaca, without education and without encouragement, found each other and began to form their individual and collective histories, having no past before the start of their conscious lives. They were a first generation, creating their own culture and language much as our prehistoric ancestors must have done. Their repertoire of stories spanned decades, covered thousands of miles, included a huge cast of characters, and held the keys to their survival. I sat spellbound as I watched the evolution of language.

My sense of awe increased with each story as I took in the tremendous detail contained in a face, the twisting of three fingers, or one perfectly timed change in posture. Each man took a turn on stage—the middle of the room— and acted out events from his life—a bullfight in Mexico City, the tragic drought that ruined the family farm, the repeated arrests by the border patrol. I could have watched their mimed conversations all night.

Ildefonso was proud of his languageless friends and very pleased to see me clearly mesmerized. He stood by my side, alternately watching the skits and observing me and my expressions. Every two minutes he nudged me and asked, "Understand? Can you understand the gestures?" He looked at his brother and his friends, at where he used to stand, then back at me. His manners were serious and business-like. He was the ringmaster, keeping the rhythm, keeping the show moving. His eyes leaped back and forth from my eyes to the storytellers, measuring my response and their performance. "See? See? Did you see that? Look!" He constantly directed my gaze to make sure I didn't miss a movement. He had to answer all those unanswerable questions I had asked years before. He wanted me to know who he had been, how he had lived, and his only experience with tribal life, with community. He knew who he was now and knew that what he had learned could not be appreciated without knowledge of where he had started.

"Look! Look! See? Do you see? It's so different, so different, completely different," he signed again and again. He looked at his friends, who stared back at him across the mysterious gulf that he had managed to cross. He was standing with his arms raised in the sign "different." One pointing hand aimed above my head, to the world of language; the other pointed across the room to his friends. Ildefonso, the conductor, stood between the cacophony of tuning instruments and the beginning of music. His two hands remained in their sign, an eye's echo, a whisper of awe—"different."

AFTERWORD

■ ■ ■

ILDEFONSO IS NOT ALONE. Unlike the few wild or abused languageless children found, hundreds of languageless deaf adults exist, most of whom receive little or no attention. Included here are stories about others who have crossed from the world of no names to the world of language, and the insights of some of their teachers.

While libraries across the country remain empty of information on languageless deaf adults, the Peace Corps actually sent a man looking for them overseas. Don Breidenthal, one of the teachers I met in Los Angeles, was sent to the Philippines to locate and teach uneducated deaf persons who had been isolated on different islands. The people he found had no language, no gestural system, and no expectation of learning. All of his fifteen students over the age of eighteen learned language with one exception, a coconut cutter who figured out that people bought his coconuts because he was different. He didn't want to change; it might hurt his business. "Learning language or anything else must be tied to human needs and desires and the student's goals," Don signed to me. "People learn what they need to learn." The most important requisite for success, he concluded, is making students aware that they *can* learn language.

> They need closeness—physical closeness, with eye contact—and opportunities where they can use language. At the school in Los Angeles, during lunch and breaks, I would sit with them [the students], instead of in the staff room. Then we were like family, using language not restricted to student roles and the classroom environment. I could say, "I'm deaf, same as you." They trusted me and witnessed an equal using language. The students improve when the teachers interact with them out of classrooms.
>
> Once a student was called in to see the director and asked, "Why aren't you learning [meaning, doing] what the teacher tells you?"
>
> "Because the teacher hates me," the student answered immediately.
>
> "What? Why do you say that?"
>
> "Look at her face!"
>
> I knew what he meant. He didn't see what she said on her hands. He saw her disapproving and hard expressions. They need closeness and contact before they see any use for language.

Later, while still in the Peace Corps, Don went to Jamaica to work with illiterate deaf adults, providing both vocational and communication-skills training. Instead of isolated individuals raised on separate islands, he found a community fluent in its own signed language. Most of them could not read, write, or perform simple arithmetic, although almost all of them had attended school from early childhood until age eighteen. Jamaica had inherited a residential school for the deaf founded by the British, who believed in strict oralist training. Signs and gesturing were forbidden, because the teachers believed signs interfered with the learning of speech and speech reading. Students who had some hearing or students who had become deaf after some years of hearing, succeeded. Congenitally deaf students, with some fortunate exceptions, remained virtually uneducated and learned little or no language skills in the classroom.

"How," I asked, "had they developed language, when none of your Filipino students had?"

"The laundry woman," he answered. Generations of deaf students passed through that school, and a few of each generation were employed as janitors, cooks, and assistants. The children picked up signs and grammar from these adult signers, adding their own vocabulary and idioms every generation. For the group he had met, the laundry woman was the head sign teacher, saving them from languagelessness.

Don reflected on his experiences at home and abroad and his ability to teach. "I didn't know the theories," he said, "I just fell into it and learned from the students. You have to know what's in their heads. One time I described the stomach and began explaining anatomy. The students were upset and asked, 'Body, divide-up, why?' They saw only dismemberment."

His ability to guess what was foremost in his students' heads helped him later when he met a deaf Vietnamese teenager who had lost most of her family on a boat after they had fled their country. She had no language, and all communication attempts failed until Don asked her about

the boat experience via pictures and mime. She answered
with a detailed gestural account. Building on this communication she was able eventually to learn her first
language.

Jane Curtan was the teacher I met while trying to find
Ildefonso, in the class very much like the one where I
had met him. In addition to twenty signing students, she
taught two deaf-blind men and five languageless adults.
A teacher's aide who had worked at the same adult education center for five years told me she saw between
five and ten languageless students every year. Even
though this happened year after year, no one ever designed a program specifically for them or developed
teaching materials. Because the languageless were considered hopeless, they were usually turned over to an
aide, but Jane decided to teach the five herself.

After I told Jane briefly about my experience with
Ildefonso and plans to write about him, she immediately
exclaimed, "Finally someone might take an interest;
there's nothing out there for these people." She had been
shocked on her first day of teaching to discover the five
languageless students, and had no idea how she would
manage such a group. She was, however, more prepared
than I had been. She had studied late language acquisition
in deaf children and taught language to older children.
She began teaching her five students according to what
she had learned about and from children. Immediately,
however, she had to change her methods and look for
new materials. None of her resources could serve adult
minds, with their very different needs and problems.

Without references or curriculum guides to help her,

she began teaching basic signs to the group while she observed, listened, and expected progress. During breaks the class all filed out to various hallways and to the cafeteria, except for the five. They used to follow the other students as far as the first hallway, where they sat on a bench in single file and stared straight ahead until class resumed. When Jane first observed their lack of even gestural communication, she wondered if they could make the leap to language. In class, they copied the signs she taught, but never used them spontaneously. For them, the signs served no purpose. "Chair," "table," and "paper" were only responses from rote when the teacher pointed to objects. They saw no use for names. Jane didn't know how to get across the significance of the symbols they practiced. "Finally, after about two weeks," she said, "I saw that Adam was sitting next to Katy and Lee next to Maria. I saw them stealing little glances at each other. Next they started passing 'notes' with drawings on them. I believe Adam started it and Lee thought it was a good idea. I never looked at what the pictures were because I felt they were personal, but I could see they were pictures."

Not long afterward the students started to sign to each other. Simple as the signs were, they represented formal communication. "Their breaks became a real social hour, and I had to herd them back to class. . . . It seems love can be a driving force for adults to learn to communicate," Jane observed.

"Wasn't it exciting to open the world to them after all those years?" I asked.

"No," she answered to my surprise. "It took forever to get them to ask questions."

I told her how impatient Ildefonso had been to find out about everything and asked her why these students had been so passive. Her response was immediate: "Experience." Those who had been protected and raised in sheltered environments had no questions. Those who had faced the frustrations and problems of life, as Ildefonso had, asked questions. Jane's oldest and most street-wise student, after he began to learn his first language at age fifty-four, brought in newspaper articles regularly for translations and explanations. His independence and inquisitiveness stood out conspicuously in her otherwise passive group. I was reminded of Ildefonso's first geography lesson and his interest in the world, a direct result of his constant need for employment and his traveling.

Jane added that her student had learned numbers and arithmetic at an amazing pace before ever learning language. Like Ildefonso, he had almost intuitively sensed a numeric system and just needed a start. Someone had given him an arithmetic book, and he had figured out many operations without being able to read one word of explanation.

I met the fifty-four-year-old student, and he immediately fingerspelled, "M-a-r-r-i-e-d," then pointed to me with a question on his face. Someone had taught him how to fingerspell this word and explained that if a woman said yes, then he was to leave her alone. For decades, he hadn't known his name, hadn't known the alphabet, and he had no formal education, yet he obediently fingerspelled this one word to every woman he met before continuing any further interaction.

Jane had another student once, an older child who had no language, who, like Ildefonso, could not understand any lesson on time. Every Sunday evening she was dropped off at a residential school for deaf children and picked up every Friday evening. Even after weeks of this pattern, she cried almost every day and could not be convinced that she would ever see her mother again. Jane tried many of the same gestural and pictoral explanations I had tried with Ildefonso but could not get across the idea of hours, days, or weeks. Finally the girl herself observed that her mother showed up when she put on the last clean outfit in her closet. She began to count the number of outfits on her shelf, associated this with waking, and eventually realized the idea of a day.

Dennis Galvan, a hearing son of Deaf parents and a native signer, became interested in langauge acquisition after working with a languageless twenty-year-old deaf Filipino. The experience piqued his interest in language acquisition, and he decided to enter a doctoral program. He originally planned to write his dissertation on adult language acquisition and study the group of languageless deaf adults involved in a program in San Francisco. The funding for the program ended, however, before he could begin. The pool of potential subjects dispersed, and there was no one to study, so he wrote his Ph.D. dissertation on late language acquisition among deaf children instead.

Dennis was originally hired to teach not language but merely information on how to ride the local train and buses, so his student could get to vocational training. Of course, Dennis introduced him to names, but the man never showed any grasp of the idea that a name or sign was standard and could be used with someone other than Dennis. He had a couple of signs—a name for father and one for ice—but he shared them with only one or two members of his family. He may have assumed that one had to invent new names with every new friend. Like Ildefonso, he survived by observing and copying. He impressed Dennis with his excellent visual-spatial skills. He could take a lock or a bicycle completely apart, fix it, and put it back together without any problems. He had learned nonverbal social behaviors and adjusted his reactions and emotions according to how he saw others react. One day, for example, the train stopped and stayed at the station for an unusually long time. He became quite agitated. Dennis couldn't explain why the train had stopped and could not tell him that everything was under control; he simply nodded his head, relaxed his shoulders, sat back comfortably, and, in his own words, "acted cool." His student understood that everything was all right and relaxed.

Also like Ildefonso, the Filipino had no idea what deafness or hearing was and did not know what was wrong with him. He wondered why people treated him differently. Specifically, he wanted to know why he was raised in the kitchen with the women and young children instead of being allowed to sit with the men. He identified with the men and wanted to belong; he could not figure out why he was not invited to join. Like Mary Ann from Ildefonso's class, he simulated visual speech acts which made no sense to him, another communication of his desire to be included.

Dennis taught him numbers so that he could read the train and bus schedules. They started with counting, first in signs, then hatches, then written numbers. The student showed great interest in money and cards, both of which became the most useful teaching methods. For hours and days, they played War, the card game, which requires counting to see who has won. The man learned to count simple numbers fairly well, but when they played Rummy, he never understood a run. He could only understand three-of-a-kind.

The most difficult task, as usual, was schedules and time. The student's only time was the present. He couldn't understand the clock and corresponding times. Dennis tried teaching the passing of time by pointing out the regular passing of trains. He and his student sat at the station and watched train after train. Dennis pointed out the 3 and the 10 on the schedule and the 3 and the 10 on the clock when the train came in. "On time," he gestured. He pointed to the next set of numbers on the schedule, then to the clock, and waited, counting off the minutes. "Late," he signed, or "early," or "on time" for train after train. Many trains later, the student could announce whether the trains were on time or not. I wonder if he thought ever after that that clocks were part of transportation systems.

Although the Filipino learned a few signs and would perhaps realize later that they worked with other signers, he never grasped the idea of language, of a system. The sign "bicycle" represented anything and everything about bicycles. He made no distinction between a verb and a noun, or plural and singular. He used one sign for train, all trains, and anything to do with a train, with a single exception—he had a separate sign for the main train station.

Since Dennis had excellent miming and visual communication skills, his student asked him questions that he had had for years. They almost all related to social behaviors that he could see but not understand. Most of them pertained to sex, women, and relationships, all of which were mysteries to him. Jane Curtan had also mentioned to me how ignorant and confused her deaf students were, including many of the signing ones, about sexuality. Since almost all the materials Jane found were for children, she had nothing to help her explain adult topics such as sexual relations, parenting, racism, and politics.

Later, Dennis met another languageless deaf adult at a Deaf party. Although the man's recently learned signing was choppy, lacked inflections, and was interrupted by occasional lapses into mime, he communicated competently. The local Deaf community had already discovered him and taken him into the fold. "We taught him signing, and now he has a car and a job," they bragged to Dennis.

When Ildefonso told me the story of how he had begged his parents to educate him, I was reminded of Jean Massieu, a deaf man born in France during the late eighteenth century. He too had desperately wanted education and had tried to convince his parents to send him to school. Unlike Ildefonso, however, he did receive years of education and began at a comparatively early age. He learned French Sign Language and French and became the first deaf teacher. He taught the Reverend Thomas Gallaudet, an American who traveled to Europe to learn how to educate deaf people and returned to found the first free school for the deaf in the United States. His youngest son, Edward Gallaudet, founded a school for deaf-mutes in Washington, D.C., which later became Gallaudet University, the only university for the deaf in the world.

In 1800, Massieu told the Society of Observers of Man his background, including a story, translated by Harlan Lane in *When the Mind Hears,* which is very similar to Ildefonso's:

> Before my education, when I was a child, I did not know how to read or write. I wanted to read and write. I often saw boys and girls going to school; I wanted to follow them, and I was very envious of them. With tears in my eyes I asked my father for permission to go to school. I took a book and opened it upside-down to show my ignorance; I put it under my arm as if to leave for school, but my father refused to give me permission, signing [gestures and signs unique to the family and not a part of any signed language] that I could never learn anything, for I was a deaf-mute. Then I wept. . . . In desperation I put my fingers to my ears and impatiently asked my father to unclog them. He answered that there was no remedy. I was disconsolate.

Fortunately, Massieu's plight came to the attention of Abbé Sicard, one of the founders of the National Institution for the Deaf in Paris, and he not only learned language but went on to teach many others.

Many more stories of successful late language acquisition can be found outside of libraries. UNICEF has a special program for uneducated adolescents which includes first language acquisition for deaf teenagers. In Paris, African deaf adolescents are regularly taught their first language at the *Institut national des jeunes sourds* (the National Institute for Deaf Youth). It is to be hoped that as this group is recognized and served there will be many more success stories in the future.

BIBLIOGRAPHY

•••

Armen, Jean-Claude. *Gazelle-Boy*. New York: Universe Books, 1974.

Austen, Paul. *City of Glass*. New York: Penguin Books, 1985.

Bragg, Bernard, and Eugene Bergman. *Lessons in Laughter*. Washington, D.C.: Gallaudet University Press, 1989.

Bridges, Thomas. *Yamana-English: A Dictionary of the Speech of Tierra del Fuego*. Rae Natalie Prosser Goodall copyright reprint: ✚ Zagier y Urruty Publicaciones Cuenca 4463, 1419 Buenos Aires, Argentina, 1987.

Bronowski, J., and U. Bellugi. "Language, Name, and Concept," *Science*, May 1970, p. 168.

Brown, Roger. *A First Language: The Early Stages*. Cambridge, Mass.: Harvard University Press, 1973.

Curtiss, Susan. *Genie: A Psy-cholinguistic Study of a Modern Day "Wild Child."* New York: Academic Press, 1977.

Douglas, Mary. *Implicit Meanings*. London and Boston: Routledge & Kegan Paul, 1975.

Furth, Hans. *Thinking Without Language*. New York: The Free Press, 1966.

Galvan, Dennis. Unpublished paper, "The Critical Period Hypothesis: Neurolinguistic and Psycholinguistic Evidence from Delayed First Language Acquisition. Berkeley: University of California, 1985.

Halliday, M. A. K. *Learning How to Mean*. London: Arnold, 1975.

Highland, C., and D. Galvin. "The Need for a Counselor-Teacher for the Deaf in Rehabilitation Settings," *Journal of Rehabilitation of the Deaf* 14 #3, Jan., 1981.

Keyes, D. *Flowers for Algernon.* New York: Harcourt, Brace & World, 1959.

Klima, E., and U. Bellugi. *The Signs of Language.* Cambridge, Mass.: Harvard University Press, 1979.

Kroeber, T. *Ishi.* Berkeley and Los Angeles: University of California Press, 1976.

La Ganga, Marla. "He's Just a Guy Called Joe: No Identity or Language, He 'Doesn't Exist' " and "At Last 'Joe' Is Somebody, Court Decides." *Los Angeles Times,* Mar. and Dec. 1982.

Lane, Harlan. *When the Mind Hears.* New York: Random House, 1984.

———. *The Wild Boy of Aveyron.* Cambridge, Mass.: Harvard University Press, 1976.

Lane, Harlan, and Richard Pillard. *The Wild Boy of Burundi.* New York: Random House, 1978.

Lenneberg, Eric. *Biological Foundations of Language.* New York: Wiley & Son, 1967.

Luria, A. R. *The Man with a Shattered World.* Cambridge, Mass.: Harvard University Press, 1972.

McKinney, Virginia. *First Language Learning in Deaf Persons Beyond the Critical Period.* Unpublished dissertation. Claremont, Calif.: Claremont Graduate School, 1983.

Milosz, Czeslaw. *The Collected Poems.* New York: The Ecco Press, 1988.

Moores, Donald. "Psychology of Deafness," *American Annals of the Deaf* 115, Jan. 1970, p. 44.

Natwick, Robyn. "Emerging Features of ASL Grammar Evidenced in Deaf Adults Whose Primary Communication Mode During Childhood Was an Idiosyncratic Gestural System." Unpublished paper. San Diego, Calif.: San Diego State University, 1985.

Neisser, Arden. *The Other Side of Silence.* New York: Alfred A. Knopf, 1983.

Padden, C., and T. Humphries. *Deaf in America; Voices from a Culture.* Cambridge, Mass.: Harvard University Press, 1988.

Sacks, Oliver. *Seeing Voices.* Berkeley and Los Angeles: University of California Press, 1989.

Schumacher, E. F. *Small Is Beautiful.* London and New York: Harper & Row, 1973.

Scouten, Edward. "The Rochester Method: An Oral Multisensory Approach for Instructing Prelingual Deaf Children," *American Annals of the Deaf* 112(2) Mar. 1967, p. 52.

Shattuck, Roger. *The Forbidden Experiment: The Story of the Wild Boy of Aveyron.* New York: Farrar, Straus & Giroux, 1980.

Timmerman, Jacobo. *Prisoner Without a Name, Cell Without a Number.* New York: Alfred A. Knopf, 1981.

Vygotsky, L. S. *Thought and Language.* Cambridge, Mass.: The MIT Press, 1962.

Whorf, Benjamin. *Language, Thought and Reality.* Cambridge, Mass.: The MIT Press, 1956.

Wilson, S., A. Nemon, E. Helman, and H. Elliott. "Communication Networks: Agents of Social Change for Immigrant and Minority Deaf Adults," from *Papers for the Second Research Conference on the Social Aspects of Deafness.* Washington, D.C.: Gallaudet College, 1986.

ABOUT THE AUTHOR

■■■

SUSAN SCHALLER was born in Cheyenne, Wyoming, graduated from San José State University in San José, California, and received a master's degree in public-health education from the University of North Carolina at Chapel Hill. She has been a teacher of American Sign Language and worked as a Sign interpreter in Los Angeles, San Francisco, and Washington, D.C. She has also worked with Indo-Chinese refugees in San Diego and in Chapel Hill. Her concern has always been with groups and individuals who receive little or no attention and how they can be encouraged toward independence. She lives in Berkeley, when she is not in Southern California nursing twin babies and a cranky Englishman.